Extraordinary MARRIAGE

God's Plan for Your Journey

Rodney and Selma Wilson

Learning Activities, CD-ROM, and Leader Guide
by Diane Noble

LifeWay Press®
Nashville, Tennessee

© 2004 • LifeWay Press®
Third Printing • October 2006
No part of this book may be reproduced or transmitted in any form or by any means,
electronic or mechanical, including photocopying and recording, or by any information
storage or retrieval system, except as may be expressly permitted in writing by the publisher.
Requests for permission should be addressed in writing to LifeWay Press®;
One LifeWay Plaza; Nashville, TN 37234-0175.

ISBN 0-6331-9787-4

This book is a resource in the Home/Family category
of the Christian Growth Study Plan.
CG-1064

Dewey Decimal Classification: 306.81
Subject Headings: MARRIAGE

Unless otherwise noted, all Scripture quotations are taken from the Holman Christian
Standard Bible®, copyright © 1999, 2000, 2001, 2002, 2003 by Holman Bible Publishers.
Used by permission.
Scripture quotations marked (CEV) are from the Contemporary English Version
Copyright © 1991, 1992, 1995 by American Bible Society. Used by permission.
Scripture quotations marked (GNT) are from the Good News Translation in Today's English
Version—Second Edition Copyright © 1992 by American Bible Society. Used by permission.
Scripture quotations marked The Message are from The Message by Eugene Patterson
© 1993, 1994, 1995, 1996, 2000, 2001, 2002 by NavPress. Used by permission.
Scripture quotations marked (NIV) are from the Holy Bible, New International Version,
copyright © 1973, 1978, 1984 by International Bible Society.
Scripture quotations marked (NKJV) are from the New King James Version.
Copyright © 1979, 1980, 1982, Thomas Nelson, Inc., Publishers.

To order additional copies of this resource: write LifeWay Church Resources Customer
Service; One LifeWay Plaza; Nashville, TN 37234-0113; fax order to (615)251-5933; phone
toll free (800)458-2772; order online at *www.lifeway.com;* e-mail *orderentry@lifeway.com;*
or visit a LifeWay Christian Store.

Printed in the United States of America

Leadership and Adult Publishing
LifeWay Church Resources
One LifeWay Plaza
Nashville, TN 37234-0175

Table of Contents

Meet the Authors

 Rodney and Selma Wilson have been married for more than 28 years and are the parents of two adult daughters, Jennifer and Natalie. Rodney is the marriage and family minister at First Baptist Church in Smyrna, TN. Selma launched the devotional magazine, *Journey* and was editor-in-chief for 5 years. Selma is currently Associate Vice President for LifeWay Church Resources.

Rodney and Selma are executive editors of *HomeLife* magazine, a national family magazine that reaches approximately 400,000 readers a month. For 20 years the Wilsons have been writing, speaking, and leading marriage ministry events.

Diane Noble wrote the learning activities, leader guide, and CD-ROM portions of this study. She is director of discipleship and women's ministries at First Baptist Church, Harrisonville, MO, where her husband David serves as pastor. Diane has an extensive background in curriculum design and development and has facilitated numerous conferences and workshops. She earned a bachelor of arts degree in education from William Jewell College in Liberty, MO, and a master of arts degree in education administration from Truman State University in Kirksville, MO. The Nobles have two grown sons, Jeff and Matt.

An ordinary night with ordinary sheep

and ordinary shepherds.

And were it not for a God

who loves to hook an "extra" on the front of ordinary,

that night would have gone unnoticed.

The sheep would have been forgotten

and the shepherds would have slept the night away.

But God dances amidst the common
and that night
He did a waltz.[1]

The God who sent an Extraordinary Savior

On an Extraordinary night

Also has a plan for you:

An Extraordinary Marriage.

---

[1]Max Lucado, *The Applause of Heaven* (Nashville: Word Publishing Group, 1999), 70.

Introduction

What's Unique about Extraordinary Marriage?

A thief comes only to steal and to kill and to destroy. I have come that they may have life and have it in abundance.
John 10:10

A car company ran a slogan that said, "On the road of life, there are passengers—and there are drivers. Drivers wanted."

Too often couples are restrained passengers stuck in the ordinary gear of neutral instead of drivers moving toward a destination. They aimlessly follow the famous Nike® slogan, "Just Do It." But you can't "just do" marriage. If you try to make it up as you go, you'll get nowhere fast.

What married couples need is a vision of where they can go as a unified driving force—and a plan for how to get there. Advertisements for the military have challenged recruits to "Be All That You Can Be." *Extraordinary Marriage* challenges couples to "Become All You Can Be In Christ."

Unlike other marriage resources, *Extraordinary Marriage* doesn't attempt to solve the typical problems of the past that plague present relationships. Rather than concentrating on past issues—or even present challenges—*Extraordinary Marriage* focuses on the realm of possibilities that exist for couples who have seen God's extraordinary vision for marriage. It paints a compelling vision of an achievable future and provides a step-by-step plan for couples to work toward that vision as drivers, not passengers.

This study looks to the future while living in the present. It provides practical guidance couples need to develop their own marriage plans for the future. It casts an extraordinary vision of God's out-of-this-world design for marital intimacy. We (Rodney and Selma) challenge you never again to settle for less than God's best but to tenaciously and steadily do whatever it takes to rise above ordinary living.

The truth of the matter is many married couples are just like those people who were physically in the presence of Jesus. Although they stood right in front of Him and literally saw Him with their physical eyes and heard His words with their physical ears, they were blind and deaf (Matt.13:13). They couldn't see beyond the present: "Isn't this Joseph's son?" they queried (Luke 4:22). They didn't see (or chose not to see) that Jesus was truly the Messiah. Their Redeemer. God's Son.

Ordinary couples are bound by the past. They live mundanely in the present with the chains of the past restraining them—exactly what Satan wants. Ordinary couples can't dream or cast a vision for the future because the past has crippled their ability to see. Often we tend to skip over the words of Jesus in Matthew 13:13, but we shouldn't. They are powerful reminders of our tendency to accept the ordinary life when the extraordinary one is so much better and accessible to those who want it!

In a world that settles for the oh-so-ordinary marital relationship, which is more akin to having a roommate than a soul mate, your marriage can be extraordinary—one that has out-of-this-world spiritual, emotional, mental, and (YES!) physical intimacy! No matter where your marriage is today, this future lies within your grasp.

Some of you are living this reality. Others may be moving toward it. Some may consider the idea a pipe dream. Actually, extraordinary marriage is God's plan for you and your mate. God does not champion the mediocre, the acceptable, the ordinary; that's not His style. Never will be. God's plan for

" 'For this reason I speak to them in parables, because looking they do not see, and hearing they do not listen or understand.' "
Matthew 13:13

The oh-so-ordinary marital relationship, is more akin to having a roommate than a soul mate.

An extraordinary marriage is the living witness of what God can do when two imperfect people focus on His perfect love.

your marriage embraces a higher love. When God created marriage, He saw it as an absolutely extraordinary way for His children to love one another and to glorify Him by living that extraordinary love out in the open for all the world to see. An extraordinary marriage is not only possible for you and your mate, it's your responsibility as followers of Christ. It's the living witness of what God can do when two imperfect people focus on His perfect love.

Wait a minute, you say; my spouse and I have a ton of imperfections and a whole heap of "ordinary living" to overcome! You're right, like the rest of us, you do. The Bible says, "For all have sinned and fall short of the glory of God" (Rom. 3:23). Left to our own devices, we sin and fall short of our intentions, much less God's best.

But here's the great news: The Bible also says God is "able to do exceedingly abundantly above all that we can ask or think, according to the power that works within us" (Eph. 3:20 NKJV). You see, the key to extraordinary marriage is to focus—not on our past, our imperfections, and our tendency to accept the ordinary—but instead, on God, His higher love, and His glory. Extraordinary marriage, by definition, describes a marriage centered in Christ the King.

Extraordinary people—and extraordinary marriages—can see beyond the present. They keep a sharp focus on life and marriage. They understand that, with God, all things are possible. They know that God takes their past experiences and uses them to make their futures better. Extraordinary couples look into the future, dream dreams, and share possibilities unhindered by the circumstances of the past because they know what the future holds. They can see it! They can live victoriously in the present with supreme confidence in the God who created them with utmost care, secure in the love of the One who gave them salvation and planned an incredible eternity for them.

For over 20 years we have shared a passion for marriage

ministry. God has given us a vision for His higher love. Our prayer is that through the pages of this resource you would see and hear God and begin or extend the plan He has for your marriage. This book has a step-by-step structure to help you do just that. When two imperfect people focus on His perfect love, an amazing thing happens: The ordinary life fades and the extraordinary life blooms!

Our prayer is that you would never settle for a mediocre relationship but instead set a course to follow the plan God has for your journey. Allow Christ to rule and reign in your marriage. Join us on this incredible journey toward a transformed marriage, toward the life and love you've always wanted—a life that begins with a plan.

Rodney & Selma

Where's Your Marriage Going?

"And he mounted his horse and rode off in all directions ..."

Know where you are headed, and you will stay on solid ground.
Proverbs 4:26 (CEV)

This expression says a lot about focus—or rather the lack of it. Do you sometimes feel that your marriage is going in many directions? A couple that allows the hectic pace of life to yank them around gets nowhere fast. There's no focal point, no compelling dream, no we're-in-this-together plan for how to get from here to there. Without focus a marriage is destined to be ordinary.

So it's no surprise when, after a few years of ordinary living, that "loving feeling" is replaced with apathy, or "You are my world" awe becomes "Who in the world are you?" animosity. Without a unifying vision, a marriage may not perish, but it certainly won't flourish. As the old saying goes, "If you aim at nothing, you're bound to hit it every time."

And a flourishing relationship is exactly what God had in mind for marriage. Marriage was created and blessed by God from the beginning of time. Throughout Scripture, God often refers to His relationship with us in the same intimate terms as a marriage relationship (Eph. 5:23-33, Rev. 19:7-9).

Read Genesis 2:24 in the margin. Underline the words that describe the intimate relationship designed for marriage.

In Genesis 2:25, we read about the first marriage and the total intimacy shared between Adam and Eve.

"Both the man and his wife were naked, yet they felt no shame."

This passage pictures a marriage relationship where a man and a woman are totally open with each other—physically, emotionally, and spiritually—without shame or blame. And with no barriers between them, a world of shared dreams lies before them!

Check the area of intimacy you believe is strongest in your marriage now.

❑ physical   ❑ emotional   ❑ spiritual

Check the area(s) of intimacy you hope will deepen.

❑ physical   ❑ emotional   ❑ spiritual

Does being a believer divorce-proof your marriage? According to a 2001 Barna survey, "Born again Christians are just as likely to get divorced as are non-born again adults. Overall, 33 percent of all born again individuals who have been married have gone through a divorce, which is statistically identical to the 34 percent incidence among non-born again adults."[1]

Sadly, Adam and Eve's flourishing dream team isn't the picture of marriage we find in today's culture, even within the walls of the church. Given these dismal statistics, George Barna stated, "It is unfortunate that so many people, regardless of their faith, experience a divorce, but especially

"This is why a man leaves his father and mother and bonds with his wife, and they become one flesh."
Genesis 2:24

unsettling to find that the faith commitment of so many born again individuals has not enabled them to strengthen and save their marriages."[2]

Unfortunate indeed. To make matters worse, these discouraging statistics don't reflect how many Christian couples avoid divorce but simply exist in "survival" mode, going through the motions with no intimacy. Why haven't these couples been tracked? Maybe because the demographic is so huge: home after home of two people living together, making a living but not a life. These couples will not divorce; they will live like two strangers that happen to occupy the same space. Stuck in marriage neutral and going nowhere.

What are some factors that contribute to these statistics?

Circle three factors you believe have the greatest effect on marriages in our culture today. Be prepared to share your thoughts with your group.

busy lifestyles	lack of direction
lack of commitment	fear of intimacy
pornography	sex before marriage
emotional barriers	me-first mentality
different interests	other?

Why are so many Christian couples accepting this ordinary life—living beneath their potential and responsibility as followers of Christ? Because God created marriage, a couple can experience genuine intimacy. How are we missing it?

The Missing Plan

For a marriage to grow from ordinary to extraordinary, we must have a plan, a mutual dream, and a sense of direction.

Otherwise, we'll find our marriages "riding off in all directions." Or, as Barna's research sadly reveals, riding off in two totally different directions.

The Bible tells us that thoughtful planning is absolutely vital to successful living.

Read Proverbs 4:26 in the margin on page 10. Put a wavy line beneath the result of knowing where you are headed.

Read Proverbs 17:24 in the margin. What keeps us from "going off in all directions"? Underline it.

We plan many areas of life. In the chart, list areas of your marriage which have lost focus or need planning. Tell why a plan would help. We've given you an example.

Area of planning	Reason plan is helpful
• *Family finances*	*Helps us set goals for buying the things we need or want.*
• _____	
• _____	
• _____	

Even when our marriage was in the newlywed stage, Selma had an uncanny sense of direction—or rather the need for it. The first four years of our marriage were the education years, when she finished her college degree, and I wrapped

An intelligent person aims at wise action, but a fool starts off in many directions.
Proverbs 17:24 (GNT)

**"I find it fascinating that most people plan their vacations with better care than they plan their lives. Perhaps that is because escape is easier."[3]
Jim Rohn
*The Treasury of Quotes***

up seminary. From seminary in Kentucky to our parents' homes in east Tennessee, we drove 300 miles. We would get a few miles down the road then—BAM!—Selma would ask a question that indicated her yearning for direction:

"Rodney, why don't we talk about where we would like our marriage to go?"

When she asked this question, Selma always had an excited but oh-so-determined look on her face — and a captive audience, I might add. She wanted to know where our relationship was headed—no surprises.

The first time Selma popped the "BAM!" question I panicked, gripped the steering wheel a little tighter, and covered my angst with no small amount of defensiveness:

"What's wrong with our marriage now?"
"Why do we have to constantly put it under a microscope?"
"Can't we just go with the flow and make it up as we go?"

The answer to that last question was, "Sure we could … at the risk of riding off in all directions." By discussing the highs, the lows and the in-betweens of our relationship, we felt we had a say-so about where our marriage was going.

So on those road trips Selma and I talked. A lot. Each time we talked, however, I felt more comfortable, and my knuckles eventually lost their death-grip on the steering wheel. In fact, I began to eagerly anticipate the BAM! question. On those trips, our car became the incubator for dreaming the future of our marriage. And once we got used to the rhythm of it all, everything flowed. Selma and I simply shared what we liked about our relationship, what needed improving, and how we could make it better. By discussing the highs, the lows, and

By discussing the highs, the lows and the in-betweens of our relationship, we felt we had a say-so about where our marriage was going.

the in-betweens of our relationship, we felt we knew the
direction we wanted to go—a say-so about where our marriage was headed—and that felt good. Which made it a lot
easier to get there.

**Place an X on each continuum below to indicate how
your "dream time" is going.**
How often do you think about the future of your marriage?

| Rarely | Occasionally | Frequently |

How often do you talk with your spouse about the future of
you marriage?

| Rarely | Occasionally | Frequently |

How often do you take action steps to accomplish a dream for
the future of your marriage?

| Rarely | Occasionally | Frequently |

Dreaming sets the stage for a couple to shape their life together. It's vital to have an atmosphere where both of you can feel
free to dream. And the reality is you can't have a dream-
come-true marriage if you don't dream together.

Dreaming together and developing a marriage plan gives your
relationship a direction. Rather than allowing the ebb and
flow of life to toss your relationship to and fro, together you
decide your future as a couple.

Few couples have a plan for their marriage, which just about guarantees it is going to ride off in all directions.

Sad but true, for most couples the marriage relationship is one of the few life journeys they don't plan. We have health-care plans, insurance plans, wedding plans, and retirement plans. We plan for the births of our children and for our deaths. We plan for the college years. We even have vacation plans. But few couples have a plan for their marriage, which just about guarantees it will ride off in all directions.

You need a marriage plan. And you need it now.

Do you have a plan for your marriage?   ❑ yes ❑ no

Do you see the advantage of having one? ❑ yes ❑ no

Are you willing to take some simple steps toward developing or improving your plan?   ❑ yes ❑ no

Developing Your Marriage Plan

If you and your mate would agree that your "marriage plan" is a bit fuzzy, how do you begin to dream of an extraordinary life together? If you're scattered in all directions, how do you begin to build a plan for your marriage?

A great place to start is to determine where you are. This book is structured so that each week helps you discern the status of an important aspect of your marriage and then dream together about where you would like to go from that point.

When you reach week six, you'll be able to put your extraordinary marriage plan in writing, simply by reviewing the notes you've made at the end of the previous weeks. Sound easy enough? Great! Let's get started. Selma and I will help you every step of the way.

Start Where You Are

Examine the following list of words. Circle any words that describe your marriage now. Space is provided to add your own words.

A great place to start is where you are in your marriage today!

Exciting	Growing	Silent	Disconnected	Hurt
Challenged	Bored	Confused	Intimate	Angry
Longing	Hoping	Frustrated	Fractured	Lazy
Energized	Ambivalent	Routine	Stagnant	Stuck
Fun	Drifting	Predictable	Scary	Lonely

_____   _____   _____

If you checked positive descriptors, great! Wouldn't you love to add a few more to your plan? If the words you circled indicate your marriage needs to grow to another level, great! That's one reason you're studying this material. Don't be discouraged. Just keep working toward the marriage you really want. Let's take some of the words you circled and begin to envision how you move from where you are to your preferred future.

List two or three words you circled that flag an area for growth. Next to each word describe the relationship you would prefer. We've given you an example.

Descriptor
- Disconnected

Preferred Future
I'd like to spend more time together doing things we enjoy and talking with each other.

Now, it's your turn.

Descriptor	Preferred Future
• _____	_____
	_____
• _____	_____
	_____
• _____	_____
	_____

When both of you have completed this activity, be prepared to share your thoughts on the Preferred Future side of the chart during Couple Talk at your next group session. Listen to your mate without comment or judgment.

Next Move
Even if your answers on the previous activity vary somewhat from those of your spouse, this tool gives you an assessment of where each of you think your marriage is today. But how in the world did it get there? Is where you are now where you hoped you would be one day? Are you living your dreams? Or, not even close?

Well, it's time for a little wisdom. Proverbs 16:16 tell us, "How much better to get wisdom than gold, to choose understanding rather than silver!" (NIV)

To better understand how God has shaped you and your spouse individually, and how that impacts your oneness as a couple, it's helpful to understand your personal and collective strengths—how God wired each of you to live Christ-focused lives. When you understand these strengths, you can better grasp how God can blend the two of you into an extraordinary one and how He can use your strengths to impact His work here on earth.

How did God wire each of you?

Marriage and family expert Dr. John Trent developed an amazing tool that enables couples to better understand their strengths and to make differences work for rather than against them. Using this assessment is a giant step in the overall journey of taking marriage from here to there, from low expectations to higher ones, from mediocre to absolutely extraordinary.

You can find the tool, Personal Strengths Assessment, on pages 27-29. Complete this fun questionnaire now. You may want to share your assessment with your spouse or bring your results to the next group session. You'll discover some exciting and energizing ways to enhance the compatibility of your marriage.

Shhh!! Assessment in process!

Have you finished your assessment tool?
Please do so now, because the remainder of this week won't make much sense if you don't. Remember, this isn't a pass-fail test. This evaluation simply shows your tendencies and traits.

Remember, this isn't a pass-fail test. This evaluation simply shows your tendencies and traits.

The New You
Now that you've gained some new insights about yourself, remember that each person is beautifully unique in Jesus Christ. No one pattern is correct, and each person typically blends these four temperaments with one being dominant. Can you begin to see what your results reveal about the way you and your spouse relate to one another? Communicate? Make decisions? Resolve conflicts?

Can you begin to see how blending your traits and those of your spouse has contributed to where you are now in your marriage? Once again, when you understand and appreciate your individual strengths and inherent temperament weaknesses, you can better grasp how God can blend the two of you into an extraordinary one. You'll be blessed to know how He can use your strengths together to impact His work.

Selma is an Otter with secondary Golden Retriever traits. You can't get more enthusiastic than my petite, effervescent wife. Selma is extremely outgoing and always "looking for the party," but, God bless her, she may overlook several details if she's planning one. On the other hand, I'm a Golden Retriever with secondary Beaver traits—a reserved but loyal guy who can analyze with the best of them but who can sometimes lose the big picture because I focus on details.

So how does the unique blend of our temperaments impact our marriage? It has made our marriage stronger. My gifts for details and organization, paired with Selma's gifts for creativity and networking, create an effective partnership in our marriage, parenting, and ministry.

Now, write at least two strengths from your personality "animal box."

My Strengths

_____   _____

_____   _____

How do you think your strengths serve to reinforce your marriage? Don't be modest! Celebrate ways you positively contribute to your marriage.

_____

_____

_____

Are you beginning to see how God can blend the two of you into an extraordinary one, and how He can use your paired strengths to impact His kingdom? Opposites not only attract, they can make a huge impact as they serve God and others.

Dream Time

After learning about each other through the assessment tool, you and your mate will know how your personality types and strengths can contribute to growth in your relationship.

Now, think about the type of marriage you want. What are some things you'd like to do with your spouse? Some places you'd like to go? You might even share some of your wildest dreams! It's quite likely you've never told your spouse some of your dreams. Now is the time to give them life by first giving them a voice. No dream is too large or too small.

On page 22, check activities that represent some of the dreams you have for your marriage. Add your own ideas in the spaces provided. Remember, there are no wrong answers. Be honest!

You will have a sharing time with your spouse at your next group session. Meanwhile, take time to think about each of the dreams you checked. Add to this list during the week.

Dream Time

I'd like for us to someday:

___ have a weekly date	___ adopt a child
___ write a book together	___ travel to Europe
___ learn to snow ski	___ drive across the country
___ build a house	___ teach in Sunday School
___ go on a mission trip together	___ take a hot air balloon ride
___ do a family mission project	___ live in another country
___ make decisions without arguing	___ operate a bed-and-breakfast
___ learn to ride a motorcycle	___ exercise together
___ take up ballroom dancing	___ buy a cabin on the lake
___ buy a red convertible	___ learn to hunt deer
___ laugh like we did when we first married	___ get away for a weekend trip once a quarter
___ _____	___ _____
___ _____	___ _____

Now to Him who is able to do above and beyond all that we ask or think—according to the power that works within you—to Him be glory!
Ephesians 3:20

Whatever your dreams for your marriage, remember, God can do more. Much more!

Do you believe God is able to do more for your marriage than you can even imagine ?
❐ yes ❐ no

Explain your answer.

_____

Are you willing to let God's power work in and through you to make your life and your marriage all He designed for you? If so, pray and ask God to take your dreams, your challenges, and the fear of the unknown that you are probably experiencing right now. Commit your hearts to Him; ask Him to perform a great work in your lives, both individually and as a couple. Remember, wherever your relationship is now, the God who created marriage is ready to take yours to the next level of purpose and intimacy. What He asks of you is that you focus your hearts on Him and agree that through Him amazing things can happen in your lives and marriage.

"For I know the plans I have for you," declares the LORD, "plans to prosper you and not to harm you, plans to give you hope and a future. Then you will call upon me and come and pray to me and I will listen to you. You will seek me and find me when you seek me with all your heart." Jeremiah 29:11-13, NIV

You may want to write a prayer to God now, or simply stop and pray a simple prayer like this one. Invite your spouse to join you, if possible.

"God, we acknowledge You as the Creator and Designer of life and marriage. We need You. We know that You have an extraordinary plan for our marriage. We commit to doing whatever it takes to reach new levels of intimacy and service. Our lives and our marriage are in your hands."

Now, kiss your spouse. You are already much closer to living the extraordinary plan God has for you because you are thinking about and dreaming dreams for the kind of marriage that only God makes possible.

What Now?

During the next few weeks, you will be choosing your marriage goals and coming up with new and exciting ideas to take your marriage to a new level of intimacy. Remember, this book is not a pass-fail. You don't need the Wilson's approval, nor do you need approval from your group leader.

However, there is Someone you want to please, even more so than your spouse. That Person is God, who deserves your highest loyalty. Pleasing God means being ready to do His will regardless of plans you have made. Let God be the leader as you embark on your journey to help your marriage honor and bring glory to Him.

On page 25 you will find the first of six worksheets you will be using in your *Couple Talk* each week. You will be transferring ideas from your dream time and other activities to this sheet. You will not work on pages 126-127 until the last session.

---

[1]"Born Again Adults Less Likely to Co-Habit, Just as Likely to Divorce," *Barna Group Online*, 6 August 2001 [cited 16 June 2004]. Available from the Internet: *www.barna.org*.

[2]Barna, "Born Again Adults." (Barna's definition of born-again Christians are those who have made a personal commitment to Jesus Christ that is still important in their life today and those who believe that when they die, they will go to heaven because they have confessed their sins and have accepted Jesus Christ as their Savior.)

[3]Jim Rohn, *The Treasury of Quotes*, Copyright ©1994 Jim Rohn International. All rights reserved.

Extraordinary Marriage Plan Worksheet

	30 DAYS ACTION PLANS	60 DAYS ACTION PLAN	90 DAYS ACTION PLAN
I. Where Is Your Marriage Going?			

How to Become a Christian

By nature, your heart runs from God and rebels against Him. The Bible calls this "sin." Romans 3:23 says, "For all have sinned and fall short of the glory of God."

Yet God loves you and wants to save you from sin, to offer you a new life of hope. John 10:10 says, "I have come that they may have life and have it in abundance."

To give you this gift of salvation, God made a way through His Son, Jesus Christ. Romans 5:8 says, "But God proves His own love for us in that while we were still sinners Christ died for us!"

You receive this gift by faith alone. Ephesians 2:8-9 says, "For by grace you are saved through faith, and this is not from yourselves; it is God's gift — not from works, so that no one can boast."

Faith is a decision of your heart demonstrated by genuine repentance and changed actions in your life. Romans 10:9 says, "If you confess with your mouth, 'Jesus is Lord,' and believe in your heart that God raised Him from the dead, you will be saved."

If you are choosing right now to believe Jesus died for your sins and to receive new life through Him, pray a prayer similar to this, accepting and thanking Him for your new life.

Dear God, I know I am a sinner. I believe Jesus died to forgive me of my sins. I now accept Your offer of eternal life. Thank You for forgiving me of all my sin. Thank You for my new life. From this day forward, I will choose to follow You.

If this expresses the prayer of your heart, we want to help you grow as a new Christian. Tell your pastor or group leader about your decision.

Personal Strengths Assessment

In each box, circle each word or phrase that describes a consistent character trait of yours when you are at home. Total the number circled in each box and multiply by two. This is your "score" for each box. Your spouse will do the same.

L	
Takes charge	Bold
Determined	Purposeful
Assertive	Decision maker
Enjoys challenges	Leader
Enterprising	Goal-driven
Competitive	Self-reliant
Firm	Adventurous

"Let's do it now!"

Double the number circled ____

O	
Takes risks	Fun-loving
Visionary	Likes variety
Motivator	Enjoys change
Energetic	Creative
Very Verbal	Group-oriented
Promoter	Mixes easily
Optimistic	Avoids details

"Trust me! It'll work out!"

Double the number circled ____

G	
Loyal	Adaptable
Non-demanding	Sympathetic
Even keel	Thoughtful
Avoids conflict	Nurturing
Enjoys routine	Patient
Dislikes change	Tolerant
Good listener	Deep relationships

"Let's keep things the way they were."

Double the number circled _____

B	
Deliberate	Discerning
Controlled	Detailed
Reserved	Analytical
Predictable	Inquisitive
Practical	Precise
Orderly	Persistent
Factual	Scheduled

"How was it done in the past?"

Double the number circled _____

Graph your temperament mix by marking your score for each temperament on the graph with a large dot. Draw a line to connect the dots.

Personality Assessment Chart

	Lion	Otter	Golden Retriever	Beaver
30				
20				
10				
0				

The following animals are used to describe the four basic temperaments:

L = Lion
Key strengths: A take charge leader, confident, purposeful; goal driven
Common weaknesses: Can be bossy, insensitive, and inflexible

O = Otter
Key strengths: Enthusiastic, friendly; mixes easily, optimistic
Common weaknesses: Exaggerates, lacks follow-through, avoids details

G = Golden Retriever
Key strengths: Loyal, good listener, sensitive, peace maker
Common weaknesses: Easily hurt, not spontaneous, indecisive, holds in personal hurt.

B = Beaver
Key strengths: Reads all instructions, precise, detailed, analytical
Common weaknesses: Afraid to break the rules, too critical, rigid, controlling[1]

Now return to page 19 and begin at The New You to complete week 1.

---

[1]Gary Smalley, *Making Love Last Forever* (Nashville: LifeWay Press®, 1996), 144-147. For a more in-depth treatment of this inventory, go to *www.ministryinsights.com/lifeway*.

Do You Know Each Other by Heart ... and Soul?

Where are you with God right now?

Therefore encourage one another and build each other up.
1 Thessalonians 5:11

O ne of the things I love about Selma is her ability to ask the right question at just the right time. It was an out-of-the-blue question that I treasure to this day. Years ago, when we were at a pivotal point in our ministry, Selma asked me,

"Rodney, where are you with God right now?"

Selma didn't ask me how my church work was going, or how my sermon skills were developing, or my interpretation of a passage of Scripture. She asked me about my personal walk with the Lord. My response wasn't glowing, as I recall. And it didn't matter; Selma wanted to know about the condition of my soul, because she cared—and that meant a lot.

Encourage each other daily, while it is still called today, so that none of you is hardened by sin's deception.
Hebrews 3:13

That key question unlocked a door for us that has remained wide open throughout our marriage. By asking about my personal walk with God, Selma gave me permission to ask her the same question. And ever so often, out of the blue, one of us will ask where the other is with God "right now."

Whatever the answer is, it's unbelievably encouraging to have the love of your life keenly interested in the health of your soul. Popping the question from time to time has helped Selma and me to cultivate spiritual intimacy. We truly know each other by heart … and soul. Daily we draw ever closer by our love for each other, Christ's love for us, and our shared and growing love for Him. It's a circle of spiritual intimacy that envelops us in an extraordinary life with God.

When was the last time you asked your spouse about his or her personal walk with God? Let this thermometer represent the "temperature" of your concern for him or her. Draw a line to match the statements to the thermometer to show if your concern is "hot" or "cold."

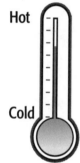

Hot

I frequently ask about his/her walk with God

I sometimes ask about his/her walk with God

I rarely ask about his/her walk with God

Cold

Spiritual Concern Thermometer

Many Christian couples rarely speak to one another in intimate terms about their personal relationship with Christ. Instead, most "spiritual" conversations focus on church activities. This is living from the outside in. But in an extraordinary marriage, life is lived from the inside out—just the opposite of what our culture dictates.

The Bible tells us, "Don't become so well-adjusted to your culture that you fit into it without even thinking. Instead, fix your attention on God. You'll be changed from the inside out..Unlike the culture around you, always dragging you

> It is unbelievably encouraging to have the love of your life keenly interested in the health of your soul.

down to its level of immaturity, God brings the best out of you, develops well-formed maturity in you" (Rom. 12:2, *The Message*).

Spiritual intimacy is the vital key to God's plan for marriage.

Spiritual intimacy, born from living life from the inside out, is the vital key to God's plan for marriage. And opening that door in your marriage will dramatically change the very soul of your relationship. Combining your personal walk with God (spiritual) with that walk with your spouse (intimacy) builds a bridge to an extraordinary marriage.

Read the following verses in your Bible. Then match each verse with the blessing we receive when we stand firm in our faith—in our walk with God.

A. Proverbs 10:25   ___ We are confirmed and sealed by God.

B. Isaiah 7:9   ___ We can really live if we stand firm.

C. 2 Corinthians 1:21-22   ___ We can weather the storms of life.

D. 1 Thessalonians 3:8   ___ God's faithful promises will be ours.

E. Hebrews 10:22-23   ___ This is the only way our marriage can stand firm.

What benefit would it bring to your marriage if you demonstrate concern and ask where your spouse's walk with God is now?_____

Would you foresee any negative reaction? If so, why?

_____

Two individual lives growing together in Christ creates openness. Trust builds, confidence in each other grows, and intimacy develops. The spiritual life feeds the intimate life.

Study the Intimate Equation below. What does it communicate to you? Check your answer.

❑ God is too far above us to ever affect our marriage.
❑ The closer each of us is to God, the closer we will be to each other.
❑ God will bless our marriage even when we are at different levels of spiritual closeness to Him.

The Intimate Equation

GOD
Jack   Jill
A

GOD
Jack
Jill
B

GOD
Jack   Jill
C

Note in Diagram A, both Jack and Jill are far away from each other—and far away from God. In Diagram B, Jack has moved closer to God, but Jill has not. So even though one spouse has moved closer to God, the intimacy between Jack and Jill is still severely limited because both are not pursuing a relationship with God. It certainly doesn't hurt the marriage for Jack to be growing spiritually, but the marriage won't thrive if Jill doesn't share this spiritual pursuit.

In Diagram B we see that each spouse plays a critical role in making spiritual intimacy a possibility. God is the granter of extraordinary intimacy, but He will not grant it unless both spouses are making the effort. Both have to truly desire this

The spiritual life feeds the intimate life.

level of intimacy and take responsibility to grow.

Diagram C is the ideal climate for spiritual intimacy. Both partners are moving closer to the Lord and to each other. In fact, growing individual relationships with God link a couple together emotionally, relationally, and spiritually.

Wherever you and your mate are now in your level of spiritual intimacy, you can go to the next level with God. He longs for you to know Him and to live daily in intimacy with Him. And He wants you to include your spouse in this circle.

Read the three verses in the margin. For each verse determine your responsibility for developing intimacy with God and His response when you obey.

Verse	My Responsibility	God's Response
Proverbs 8:35	_____	_____
Isaiah 55:3	_____	_____
James 4:8	_____	_____

Getting to the Core Issue

The lack of spiritual intimacy may not fragment a relationship overnight. It may take years of surface religion to leave a marriage noticeably depleted of growth and vitality. On the outside, everything may look good, but behind the doors of many marriages, the relationship is dangerously brittle.

Take Jonathan and Amanda for example. They have been married for 19 years and have three great kids. Jonathan teaches a Sunday School class, and Amanda coordinates their church's Web site from her stay-at-home mom office.

Wherever you and your mate are now in your level of spiritual intimacy, you can go to the next level with God.

For the one who finds me finds life and obtains favor from the Lord.
Proverbs 8:35

Pay attention and come to Me; listen, so that you will live.
Isaiah 55:3

Draw near to God, and He will draw near to you.
James 4:8

To the rest of the world, and to many in the church, Jonathan and Amanda's marriage looks quite spiritual. But there is an emptiness that is reaching the point of crisis. For 16 years Jonathan and Amanda have been gradually moving away from each other and from intimacy with God. They live in the same house but have no life in their relationship—not with each other and not with God. They embrace a surface spirituality, but there is no connection to a growing, personal walk with Jesus Christ, or a shared walk with each other.

Jonathan and Amanda speak a lot of surface banter but never dive below to share from their hearts. They practice religion but not relationship. They focus their time and energy on usual "activities" rather than on becoming more like Christ.

Read the following verses in your Bible. Explain the key thought of each verse. We've given two examples.

Verse   **Key Thought**

Psalm 16:11   There is abundant joy in God's presence.

Colossians 2:8 Thinking like the world offers empty deceit.

Psalm 86:5

Psalm 119:65

Indicate whether each key thought leads to a full life by circling the Scripture reference. If the thought leads to emptiness, cross out the reference.

He Wrote the Book on Love
Some may think their marriages have been devoid of spiritual intimacy far too long to ever become vibrant again. But God

If anyone is in Christ there is a new creation; old things have passed away, and look, new things have come.
2 Corinthians 5:17

delights in taking the impossible and making it possible. He's the Creator of marriage, and He knows just what our marriages need to thrive. He wants you and your spouse to get to know Him more personally—and jointly—so He can teach you what He knows about loving relationships.

During my freshman year in college, I (Rodney) struggled through a required math course entitled Introductory Mathematics Analysis. The following summer I saw an old high school friend who had taken the same course at a different school using the same text book. He sailed through the class! He was actually excited as we discussed the course, which stirred my curiosity. I told him of my struggle and asked him why he had done so well. He informed me that his professor was the author of the textbook. "The professor made everything so clear because he created those ideas. You just had a teacher, Rodney; I had the author!"

What a resounding truth for marriages! Jesus spoke of marriage saying, "What God hath joined together ..." (Mark 10:9), telling us that He is the Creator of marriage. Getting to know the Creator will help you and your spouse discover what marriage should become.

When you have spiritual intimacy with Him, He'll make the way clear because He literally wrote the book on love. The key to an extraordinary marriage is to first seek a growing personal relationship with Him. Matthew 6:33 says, " 'Seek first his kingdom and his righteousness and all these things will be given to you as well' " (NIV).

Seeking and knowing God the Creator individually is the first priority, if you want to have an extraordinary marriage.

If you want to have an extraordinary marriage, the first priority is seeking and knowing God the Creator of marriage individually. When you both have spiritual intimacy with God, it infuses your marriage with oxygen so your relationship can breathe deeply and become extraordinary—just as He planned from the beginning.

Read John 15:9-12 in your Bible. What are the benefits of staying connected with Jesus? Check one or more.

❑ We will remain in Christ's love.
❑ We can avoid heartache and problems in life.
❑ We will have joy—complete joy.
❑ We can love each other like Christ loves us.

Christ wants us to have an intimate and abiding relationship with Him. Apart from Him we cannot fully experience His love or the joy He wants to bring into our lives. As believers we will continue to experience problems in life, but we have a joy that lifts us above our circumstances. With His joy in our hearts we can love one another like Christ loves us.

The Strong Foundation of Salvation
If you've been building your marriage on shaky ground, ask God to rebuild your lives and your marriage on a new firm foundation. Psalms 127:1 says:

> *Unless the LORD builds the house,*
> *its builders labor in vain.*

Two lives joined as one and centered on Jesus Christ form the cornerstone of an extraordinary marriage. But sin must be removed before this cornerstone can be set in place. The Bible says we're all born as sinful beings who "fall short of the glory of God" (Rom. 3:23). Because of His love for you, God placed your sins on the sinless shoulders of His only Son. Jesus' sacrifice on the cross made it possible for you to have a personal and eternal relationship with God.

The Bible says, "While we were still sinners Christ died for us!" (Rom. 5:8). All you need to do is receive this gift of forgiveness and grace by faith. Ephesians 2:8-9 says, "For by grace you are saved through faith, and this not from yourselves; it is God's gift—not from works, so that no one can boast."

If you would like to receive the gift of eternal life with God and begin to live a life and a marriage that has Jesus Christ at the center, pray a prayer similar to this:

> *Dear God, I know I'm a sinner. I believe Your Son Jesus died to save me from my sins. I ask Your forgiveness of those sins and accept Your offer of eternal life. Thank You for forgiving me of all my sins. From this day forward, I choose to follow You and call You Lord of my life. Amen.*

Share this decision with your mate and then with a local church minister or your group leader. Connect with a nearby church to become part of a large family of believers who will help you grow in your faith. Incidentally, this brief focus on how to become a Christian isn't a digression. It has everything to do with how to have the best marriage possible.

Good tools help you in your beginning steps as a new Christian—or any Christian. Your local Christian bookstore will have many resources to help you grow. Also, page 26 is a concise summary of how to become a Christian. Share it with others God brings your way.

Start Here
Regardless of whether you've been a follower of Christ for a day or decades, combining a growing spiritual life with intimacy in your marriage may still seem difficult. Let's explore how you can get intimate about spiritual matters.

First, let's be clear: intimacy is more than sex. A lot more. Intimacy is openness, letting your mate see the real you. Selma and I like the saying that intimacy is "into me, see." It involves risking, trusting, and having assurance that your trust is well-founded. Does that include sex? Sometimes. But sex is only part of the equation. (Hang on, guys, we'll get to sex in the next chapter!)

You've learned that the spiritual side of your marriage begins with salvation, but it grows through your on-going relationship with Jesus Christ or your "walk" with God. So it's time to pop the question: Where are you with God right now?

Where are you with God right now?

Read the following verses. Put a check under the column that indicates how well you personally follow the instructions in each verse.

	Rarely	Occasionally	Often
Ephesians 6:18			
I Peter 4:10			
1 John 1:7			
1 John 2:5			

Based on your responses, circle these spiritual disciplines you need to strengthen.

Bible study   prayer   worship   serving others

Your personal walk with God needs to be strong to ensure that spiritual intimacy with your spouse is possible.

Using the same words from the previous exercise, indicate how often you share these experiences with your spouse by underlining one or more.

During *Couple Talk*, agree on areas that need to be strengthened during this study.

Next Steps: The Elements of Spiritual Intimacy

Since the spiritual aspect of your two lives drives the quality of intimacy in your marriage, let's look at some of the things you can begin to do today that will help you build an extraordinary marriage full of spiritual intimacy.

Individual Quiet Time

Any spiritual intimacy your marriage experiences depends on your own personal walk with the Lord. You must carve time out of your busy days to be alone with God and His Word and to talk to Him. More importantly, let Him speak to you.

Selma and I highly recommend you journal what God is telling you during your times with Him. Journaling is writing specific requests, praises, or confessions that will help you provide a powerful way to share God's grace with your spouse, children, and others. Spiritual intimacy begins with you and God and then moves to shared intimacy with your marriage.

Spiritual intimacy begins with you and God and then moves into shared intimacy within your marriage.

What do you need to do to develop a consistent quiet time?

❑ Create a quiet space. Where could that be? _____

_____

❑ Wake up 10-15 minutes earlier in the morning.

❑ Miss one evening activity and replace it with a quiet time.
❑ Inform the family of your personal time and encourage
  minimal disruptions.

**How frequently will you commit to quiet time?
Remember some is better than none! Check your
answer.**

❑ daily　　　　❑ 4 times a week　　❑ 2 times a week

To help you develop the discipline of a daily personal quiet
time, devotionals for husbands and wives are located on the
CD-ROM in the Leader Kit. We suggest that each spouse use
these individual devotionals to begin cultivating a growing
personal relationship with Christ.

Couple Quiet Time
The best way to unite spiritually is to share out of the over-
flow of what God is doing and saying in your individual quiet
times. Pull out that journal and share with your spouse a
verse of Scripture or a truth you feel God impressed upon
you. Share what God has been teaching you in your personal
quiet time. Use these questions to jump start conversations
with one another about intimate spiritual issues.

1. What are the core truths of this Scripture passage?
2. How do these truths apply to our marriage?
3. What steps can we take together to make these truths
   become even more consistent in our marriage?

Eventually, you and you spouse may want to read the Bible
together. But remember, longer is not always better. Sharing
a verse or a paragraph can be much more powerful than reading an entire chapter. In the early years of their marriage,
authors Les and Leslie Parrott used to fight over who would

read the Bible each night. They each wanted the other to read so the listener could doze off!

Unifying Prayer

Praying together, a unifying force, is an extremely intimate step for a husband and wife. It requires trust, a willingness to bare all to God, and discretion in sharing with one another. Praying can forever bind two souls together. If you want an extraordinary marriage, prayer is your most powerful resource. However, if you use prayer as a weapon such as "Lord, tell Harry to help more around the house," you will soon cease praying as a couple.

Commit to pray together for your marriage. On each slice of the circle, write something specific you will pray for during this study.

In Matthew 18:19 Jesus says, " 'Again, I assure you: If two of you on earth agree about any matter that you pray for, it will be done for you by My Father in heaven.' " If you and your spouse regularly pray together for an extraordinary marriage—joining your hands, your hearts, and your souls— God will answer those prayers in extraordinary ways.

Other verses to help you develop a healthy prayer life:
Philippians 4:6
Colossians 4:2
1 Thessalonians 5:17
1 Timothy 2:8
Hebrews 4:16

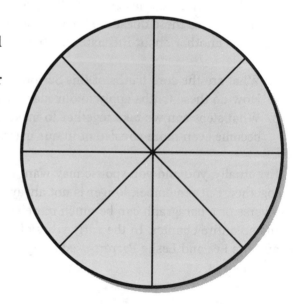

In your private conversations with God, pray daily for your spouse and specific needs in his/her life. Become your spouse's #1 prayer partner and share together how God answers those prayers. Before your spouse walks out the door each morning make it a habit to ask, "How can I pray for you today?" Knowing you are lifting each other up to God throughout the day is both edifying and unifying.

Ministry Response
Finally, pray that God will use your marriage to advance His kingdom—but be prepared for amazing opportunities to develop if you do! There is nothing more powerful in your journey toward spiritual intimacy than to allow God to use you and your marriage for kingdom purposes!

Selma and I minister together as we lead marriage enrichment events and teach studies in our church to build stronger families. What ministry activity could you participate in as a couple? We've given suggestions later in this chapter. For now, dream. Just let God speak to you in His own way and time.

Benefits of Spiritual Intimacy
Experiencing true spiritual intimacy with your spouse provides security in an uncertain, frequently-changing, divorce-is-common kind of world. It's an opportunity to keep God right where He belongs—at the heart of your marriage. Spiritual intimacy gives you confidence in who you are in Christ, individually and as a team.

Such confidence creates awareness that you and your spouse are joined for a purpose—to serve God. God's kingdom reaches to every corner of the globe, to every lost person, and to your next door neighbor. That mission and ministry agenda gives an extraordinary marriage its true focus.

**Denying ourselves the privilege of the intimacy that was so extravagantly purchased for us at the Cross is to leave ourselves struggling with the aloneness that the distance inflicts on our souls.[1]
Joseph M. Stowell
*Coming Home***

If you are not experiencing spiritual intimacy with God, you'll never know the potential of oneness and intimacy with your spouse.

If you are not experiencing spiritual intimacy with God, you'll never know the full potential of oneness and intimacy with your spouse. Everything else you do (seeking physical or emotional intimacy, conflict management, and so on) will just be taking baby steps in your marital journey; whatever progress you make won't last. When the chaos and the pace of life hit, the baby steps won't be enough. But when you bond together through intimacy with God, the world can whirl out of control, but you, your marriage, and your home will stand. Jesus spoke of this in Matthew 7:24-27 (NIV).

Everyone who hears these words of mine and puts them into practice is like a wise man who built his house on the rock. The rain came down, the streams rose, and the winds blew and beat against that house; yet it did not fall, because it had its foundation on the rock. But everyone who hears these words of mine and does not put them into practice is like a foolish man who built his house on the sand. The rain came down, the streams rose, and the winds blew and beat against the house, and it fell with a great crash.

For You are my rock and my fortress;
You lead and guide me
because of Your name. Psalm 31:3

Underline the statement that best describes the foundation of your marriage.

1. Oops. I feel a little shaky. Take cover!
2. My sand looks pretty solid to me.
3. Our foundation is still in question. We are mixing in a few pebbles with the sand.
4. Our foundation is secure. We're building a marriage and family based on God.

You and your spouse can know each other intimately —by heart and soul. Your love for each other, Christ's love for you, and your shared and growing love for Him can draw you closer and closer each day. Build your marriage on this strong foundation of spiritual intimacy—and watch the extraordinary life begin.

Now that you've committed to a firm foundation for an extraordinary marriage, remember that we promised we would get to the subject of sex. Well, another benefit of spiritual intimacy in marriage is that it often leads to the physical kind—which is wonderful. That's a natural progression which can greatly enhance a couple's sex life. Within the home of a married couple, an exhilarating sexual relationship is a phenomenon that makes God smile. And next week we'll explore the physical side of marriage—and how it can be extraordinary too.

Intimacy on Warp Speed? Can It Happen?
Selma and I have to smile as we end this chapter. Writing this book in the middle of "doing life" has created a broad range of emotions — primarily exhaustion. This past month has been packed full of counseling appointments, two major marriage and family enrichment events at our church, company at our house (for months!), and Selma's getting a major virus! Selma's father had emergency open heart surgery and one daughter graduated from high school. The other daughter received an honors award at her college. Of course, we went to the banquet.

One Sunday after church, Selma noticed I wasn't my normal self. I was exhausted—physically, emotionally, and spiritually. Selma and our daughter, Natalie, were excited about the morning service. I have to admit I hadn't gotten a thing out of worship because my heart and mind were distracted.

Selma gave me permission to feel without judging, and she planted me on the couch with the remote control, a pillow, a glass of iced tea, my favorite snacks, a ballgame, and the admonition "Rest!" (Wives, this will work every time to renew your husband's strength.) She then cancelled a small group Bible study we were going to have in our home that night, and added, "No writing today!"

I gratefully obeyed. By the next day, I was physically, emotionally, and spiritually renewed! I thank God for a partner who let's me be me, weaknesses and all. That kind of intimacy is extraordinary!

Dream Time
It's time to envision that preferred future for your marriage. You've looked at several ways to strengthen your intimacy with God and with each other. With these skills you are now ready to dream your personal dreams and then share them with your spouse in *Couple Talk*.

Agreement is not nearly as important as listening, asking questions, letting new ideas get absorbed into your heart and soul. So, as you talk, let go of your presuppositions about your list or that of your husband/wife. I hope Selma's gift to me on my weary Sunday afternoon can inspire you to gift your partner with support and flexibility.

We want to leave you with this famous quote by Mark Twain.

Twenty years from now

you will be more disappointed

by the things you didn't do

than by the ones you did do.

So, throw off your bowlines.

Sail away from the safe harbor.

Catch the trade winds in your sails.

Explore.

Dream.

Discover.[2]

---

[1]Joseph M. Stowell, *Coming Home: The Soul's Search for Intimacy with God* (Chicago: Moody Press, 1998), 29.
[2]Mark Twain (1835-1910), *The Quotations Page,* [cited 30 June 2004]. Available from the Internet: *www.quotationspage.com.*

DREAM TIME

Study the list below. Check some of the activities you would like to do together. Additional spaces have been provided to continue dreaming.

I'd like to someday:

- ☐ take a mission trip together
- ☐ host a neighborhood Bible study
- ☐ journal regularly
- ☐ pray together
- ☐ memorize scripture together
- ☐ have consistent quiet times
- ☐ read a devotional book together
- ☐ lead someone to the Lord
- ☐ share our faith with someone of another religion
- ☐ mentor a new believer
- ☐ budget my energy to give spiritually to my mate
- ☐ take a Bible conference cruise

—— _____

—— _____

—— _____

In the next group session, you will have an opportunity to share this list with your spouse.

I hope you will bring to the *Couple Talk* each week an open mind, a willing spirit, an unconditional love, and a heart for the Lord. Brush away your agendas. Be a team player, on God's team.

Extraordinary Marriage Plan Worksheet

	30 DAYS ACTION PLANS	60 DAYS ACTION PLAN	90 DAYS ACTION PLAN
2. Spiritual Intimacy			

Week Three

Is Your Sex Life Healthy?

A gift ... and a responsibility

Has not the Lord made them one? In flesh and in spirit they are his. And why one? Because he was seeking godly offspring. So guard yourself in your spirit, and do not break faith with the wife of your youth.
Malachi 2:15, NIV

Years ago, Selma and I were leading a marriage enrichment seminar entitled "Sex in the Middle Years." Most of those who attended were 50 plus; that surprised us, given the fact few of us live to be 100! But we were absolutely thrilled that the couples in the seminar were quite expressive. When we were discussing how to keep sex interesting throughout the years, someone offered, "Who says it has to always be in the bedroom?" An older man, whom we later learned was a pastor, replied, "Because they'll arrest you if you try that at Kroger!" His comment gave new meaning to the slogan, "Let's go Krogering."

Talking so openly about sex in that seminar was not only a refreshing adventure but also a sobering reminder that honest conversations about sexual intimacy are rare for the Christian couple. Sure, in public most married couples will laugh about sexual issues, but when they get behind closed doors, far too many clam up.

Isn't it ironic that so many in the secular world openly talk about sex, but most Christian couples have difficulty discussing it with each other? Since sex was designed and celebrated by God, you would expect quite the opposite.

On the line, put an X to describe how open you are to discussing your sex life with your mate?

Shut   Open

Although the subject of sex leaves many Christians tongue-tied, the Bible has a lot to say about it. And it doesn't mince words. Sexual love is to be experienced only between a husband and his wife. Let's look at key verses in 1 Corinthians 7:3-5 (*The Message*).

> *It's good for a man to have a wife, and for a woman to have a husband. Sexual drives are strong, but marriage is strong enough to contain them and provide for a balanced and fulfilling sexual life in a world of sexual disorder. The marriage bed must be a place of mutuality—the husband seeking to satisfy his wife, the wife seeking to satisfy her husband. Marriage is not a place to "stand up for your rights." Marriage is a decision to serve the other, whether in bed or out. Abstaining from sex is permissible for a period of time if you both agree to it, and if it's for the purposes of prayer and fasting—but only for such times. Then come back together again. Satan has an ingenious way of tempting us when we least expect it.*

Complete Paul's key points by adding key words.

1. Marriage is designed to contain our natural God-given

_____ drives.

2. God's plan for marriage provides for a balanced and

_____ sexual relationship.

3. The sexual relationship in marriage is to be mutually

_____ to both husband and wife.

4. Marriage, is a conscious _____—an act of
the will—to serve the other.

5. God wants _____ to be consistently given; not
withheld as a act of neglect or manipulation.

6. Healthy sex in marriage helps us resist Satan's

_____.

Wow! Do you get it? Sex—giving to each other physically—is
a vital element of an extraordinary marriage. To summarize
these verses from God's Word: "HAVE SEX!" Remember the
experience is emotional and relational as well as physical.

The quality of your sexual intimacy is a reflection of your total relationship.

Given that biblical edict, if you want a quick evaluation of the
health of your marriage, look at your sex life. The quality of
your sexual intimacy is a reflection of your total relationship.
And the lack of physical intimacy is often a symptom of
some other issues.

Take Karen and Bob, for example. After speaking with them,
it didn't take me (Rodney) long to discern serious barriers in
their marriage. I felt the distance between them, both in body
language and attitude. Spiritually, Karen and Bob were empty.

After discussing that aspect of their relationship, I asked them, "How's your sex life?" I think my question floored them. They looked up in surprise, glanced nervously at each other, and then looked down. Karen mumbled, "I can't remember the last time we had sex that was fulfilling to me." Bob thought for a moment longer, then said, "We never talk about it, but I can't remember the last time we had sex!"

Karen and Bob's sexual relationship was practically non-existent, which is always a warning flare off the bow of the marriage boat. The fact that they only glanced at each other and preferred looking at the floor when I inquired about their sex life told me it was a subject they avoided. It also signaled an emotional void. Karen and Bob lived in the same house, shared the same last name and bed, but lacked true intimacy.

A void in sexual intimacy signals a probable emotional void as well.

When thinking about physical intimacy in your marriage, which of the following contributes to your sense of emotional security? Check one or more.

- ❑ touching
- ❑ timing
- ❑ talking
- ❑ teasing
- ❑ testing
- ❑ togetherness
- ❑ trusting
- ❑ other? _____

Two Levels of Sexual Intimacy
Like many other married couples, Karen and Bob failed to view sex on both of these levels:
1. having sex;
2. talking about sex.

Our culture bombards us with wrong messages about sex that are contrary to God's Word.

Basically the secular world sees only one dimension of sex—the physical act. In other words, let's strip away all the special emotional and relational features of sex that we as humans are privileged to experience and just focus on the physical act, like animals do. Our culture bombards us with wrong messages about sex—messages that are contrary to God's Word.

List examples of how these aspects of our culture shape people's beliefs that sex outside of God's plan for marriage is acceptable—even desirable.

• Television—

• Music—

• Magazines—

• Radio talk shows—

• Commercials—

• Peer pressure—

We're sure you found many examples! While culture can distort the sanctity of the marriage relationship, God deepens it by consecrating physical intimacy between a man and wife.

Well, there's intimacy, and then there's intimacy. Physical sex is clearly one level of intimacy—the most obvious and tangible level. However, it's emphasized so much today that many, including Christian couples, think physical sex is the ultimate experience in marital intimacy, and perhaps even life itself. In the groundbreaking book *Sheet Music,* Dr. Kevin Leman writes, "Sex is about the quality of your entire love life, not just the alignment of your bodies."[1]

Well said! Extraordinary sex between a husband and wife requires emotional and relational intimacy. Couples need to open up and discuss this very intimate aspect of their relationship. Sex is indeed a precious gift from God, but it's also a responsibility. Each mate has the responsibility to make it the best experience they can for the other. And that requires speaking about the matter together. In detail. And often.

In the blanks, write a C (comfortable) or a U (uncomfortable) if you were in the following situations.

____ discussing the topic of sex with your spouse
____ discussing the topic of sex with your child
____ discussing your own physical intimacy needs
____ expressing likes and dislikes in your physical intimacy
____ asking for a change in any routines of physical intimacy
____ granting requests for changes in any physical routines
____ being asked by your spouse to read from a Christian book or magazine helpful articles about sex
____ listening to teaching and preaching about sex

There are many couples today, like Bob and Karen, who have NEVER discussed their sex life with each other. Are you and your spouse among the many? Have you gone through your marriage assuming your mate likes to be touched there, and that he or she prefers a certain position? Are you operating under the philosophy: "This is how we've done it for 20 years! Why change now?" If so, rethink and revive your sex life, which requires some communication.

With old assumptions, physical intimacy becomes extremely limited and ultimately stifled. But God planned just the opposite for you and your spouse: He wants you to experience this part of your lives abundantly!

> Sex is indeed a precious gift from God, but it's also a responsibility.

In your Bible find Song of Songs (Song of Solomon) and read these verses from God's Word. Then draw a line to the matching act of marital intimacy painted in that Scripture.

God's Word   **The Picture**

1: 4   • The couple spends the night experiencing intimacy.

1:13-14   • They savor the sweetness of their kisses.

2: 5-6   • They are eager to experience physical intimacy.

4:10-11   • Their embraces are tender and intimate.

Go ahead—read the entire book of Song of Songs! You may gather some great ideas! God is good, isn't He?

If you want an extraordinary marriage, act now to break the ice, take the risk, and discuss the subject of sex with your mate. If you feel like pulling the bedcovers over your head at just the thought of such a discussion, relax. Selma and I are going to help you and your spouse "pillow talk" with two simple exercises. Then, later in this chapter, we'll help you dream together about making some helpful changes to the physical aspect of love.

Pillow Talk Exercise # 1

Take this simple T (true) F (false) test, writing your answers in your own study book or on separate sheets of paper. Do not compare answers with your spouse.

Dream together about making some helpful changes to the physical aspect of love.

56

T	F	1. Regarding sexual readiness, most women are like microwaves and most men are like crock pots.
T	F	2. Having sex three times per week indicates a healthy sex life.
T	F	3. Your mind is your most powerful sex organ.
T	F	4. How the wife/husband views herself/himself doesn't affect their sex life.
T	F	5. Sex is important to men and romance is important to women.
T	F	6. Spontaneous sex is the best.
T	F	7. Planned sex is the best.
T	F	8. What takes place outside the bedroom has little effect on sex.
T	F	9. Sex is best when the needs of both the husband and the wife are met.
T	F	10. Spiritual and sexual are two unrelated terms.

When both of you have completed this test, take turns reading aloud the explanations that we have given for our own answers. These explanations have been written "in your personal voice," which will help you begin to feel more comfortable verbalizing sexual issues.

Explanation to True / False Activity
Remember, read these answers and explanations aloud to one another. They are clearly marked for the husband or wife.

1. Regarding sexual readiness, most women are like microwaves and most men are like crock pots.. FALSE

Her Read: One of the keys to greater sexual intimacy is understanding that you and I, as a man and woman, tell sexual time very differently.

For Women	For Men
Sex is about 24 hours.	Sex is about 15 minutes.
The clock begins when we get out of bed in the morning.	The clock begins when we go to bed at night.
Timing includes all five senses.	Timing means "it's time!"

A Note from Selma: **Ladies, don't be shy about telling your man you need more time than he does to get focused and ready for sexual intimacy. When you understand your husband's immediate readiness, and he understands that timing is critical for you, your cooperation and teamwork will lead you to a new level of intimacy.**

2. **Having sex three times per week indicates a healthy sex life. FALSE.**

His Read: **We should keep the counting out of the bedroom. The number of times we have sex isn't the critical factor; the focus should be on meeting each other's needs.**

A Note from Rodney: **Sure, the Bible says husbands and wives should have sex (1 Cor. 7:3), but it doesn't say how often. Frequency is a decision of the individual couple and will vary throughout life depending on numerous factors.**

3. **Your mind is your most powerful sex organ. TRUE**

Her Read: **Our attitudes about life, self, and each other are critical to a healthy sex life. Outside attitudes about work, children, neighbors, and extended family can impact the intimacy we share with each other. Let's do a mental check** up: How's your attitude? How's mine? Where do we each put our focus? Answers to these questions make all the difference in our relationship, especially as it relates to our sex life.

A Note from Selma: Establish the 80/20 rule in your relationship, agreeing that 80 percent of what each spouse does is great, but admitting 20 percent needs some work. Focus on the 80 percent to increase the odds that you'll both leave tension and criticism outside the bedroom.

4. How the wife/husband views herself/himself doesn't affect their sex life. FALSE

His Read: Self-esteem is another critical factor of marital intimacy. What happens if you gain weight or I begin to lose my hair? We need to learn to affirm and help each other accept ourselves without making cutting, hurtful remarks toward each other. As we focus on how each grows as individuals, the intimacy within our relationship will also grow.

A Note from Rodney: To cultivate healthy self-esteem continue to discover who you are in Jesus Christ. In Him, we are forgiven, made new, and empowered by the Holy Spirit. That's a secure foundation for self-worth.

5. Sex is important to men and romance is important to women. TRUE

Her Read: In survey after survey, sex will be one of the top three critical needs of men. It seldom even makes the list of critical needs of women; those slots belong to romance and affection. God made you and me uniquely different, and those differences create the best opportunity to live in a servant role as we focus on meeting each other's needs.

Self-esteem is a critical factor of marital intimacy.

In the busyness of life, we must make our physical intimacy a priority.

A Note from Selma: Ephesians 5 clearly shows the differences between men and women. God designed men to have a leadership role in the home, thus the need for respect and esteem. God designed women to be loved and cherished, thus the need for romance and affection. It's critical that each of you shares how your spouse can best show respect, esteem, romance, and affection in your unique marriage. For me, romance is the surprise of a single rose, a card for no reason, or a cup of coffee shared when I first wake up. For other women it would be something different.

6&7. Spontaneous sex is the best. Planned sex is the best. Both are TRUE.

His Read: Boredom will kill our sexual intimacy. A deep and fulfilling passion is a lifelong possibility that we must nurture. How do we add passion to our marriage? By being creative and spontaneous, by planning new adventures, taking risks, or going out of our way to keep the physical intimacy alive. But we also need to plan for sexual times together. In the busyness of life, we must make our physical intimacy a priority. Reserve time on the calendar; block off time where we save our energy to give to each other physically. Planning will add excitement and expectation to our relationship.

A Note from Rodney: With today's pace of life, sexual intimacy with your spouse must be an intentional desire, not just an afterthought. You don't get to an extraordinary sex life unless you determine you won't settle for anything less. Dr. James Dobson once said, "Tired bodies make for tired sex." A time-consuming, energy-sapping daily schedule will not allow a good sex life to just happen.

This is one area that really hits home for Selma and me. I'm much more spontaneous. But Selma's favorite setting is a romantic getaway where she can take her mind off work, maintaining a home, and the endless to-do lists of life. Hotel getaways are not always possible for couples—especially with preschoolers. Think of some other options. In order to make some alone time, take someone's children for the weekend and let them keep yours the following weekend.

8. What takes place outside the bedroom has little effect on sex. FALSE

Her Read: What takes place outside our bedroom has everything to do with our sexual intimacy. For example, sex begins in the morning over breakfast with a smile, a touch, a kiss, and tender good-byes. Keeping these moments tender will cultivate respect for each other and can make a major difference in our sexual intimacy. However, if the other 23 hours of our day are packed with the busyness of life, unresolved conflict, or the stress of debt, it will be hard to turn that "stuff" off and experience the sexual intimacy that God designed for us.

A Note from Selma: Be intentional about your marriage. Don't let the noise of living drown out the gift of intimacy God has given you. Guard your mind, your heart, and your energy. All of these affect the issue of faithfulness to your spouse and are a major factor in marital intimacy.

9. Sex is best when both partners have their needs met. TRUE.

His Read: God designed marriage and sex to meet needs. Today, let's commit to really study each other, to know each other's likes and dislikes. Let's begin to share our sexual needs openly and honestly with each other. Seeking to please each other is a recipe for mutual satisfaction.

A Note from Rodney: God didn't make a mistake when he designed man and woman so differently. Our differences give us an opportunity to put our own needs aside and to focus on the needs of our mate. In doing so, we grow to be more like Christ. One of the adventures of an extraordinary, Kingdom-focused marriage is learning more about your mate and learning to put his or her needs before your own.

10. One's spiritual life and sex life are two unrelated areas. FALSE.

Her Read: Our ability to put each other's needs before our own really depends on our intimacy with the Creator and Designer of marriage. The closer you and your spouse are to Him, the greater your physical intimacy will be.

> **The closer you and your spouse are to God, the greater your physical intimacy will be.**

A Note from Selma: There's no feeling like the one you get when you are making love to your mate and you know that God, the Creator of sex, is smiling on you. That's the "spiritual" smiling on the "physical." An extraordinary experience indeed!

Pillow Talk Exercise # 2
See, talking about sex wasn't so hard! Quite likely, you just spent an hour learning new things about one another. Now that you're a bit more comfortable with pillow talk, here's an exercise that can really take you to a more intimate level. It's Les and Leslie Parrott's XYZ Formula, which goes like this:

In situation ____X____,
when you do ____Y____,
then I feel ____Z____.[2]

For example, using the XYZ Formula, you can say to your wife: "When I express a desire to have sex with you, (situation X), and you turn me down by saying, 'Is that all you ever think about?' (Y), then I feel like my needs are not important to you (Z)."

Or you could say to your husband, "When you want to have sex (situation X), and you take the time to set the mood in our bedroom (put on some music, light some candles, etc.) (Y), then I feel that you care about me as a person (Z)."[3]

To make the most of this exercise, in advance and separately, brainstorm "X." Make a list of various situations that you would like to discuss with your mate. Be specific as to any area of sex you want to address. Open and honest communication is the guiding light here! This simple exercise is a great icebreaker that can enable you to discuss this important part of your marriage relationship more in depth. Remember, needs may change over time. Don't assume that "getting it right" now will last you a lifetime.

Don't expect always to think and act in ways that will please your mate. Some days may feel more intimate than others, but that is the nature of human relationships.

Read this quote from Alan Loy McGinnis in his book,
The Romance Factor.

> All love relationships are something of a dance in which two people are constantly moving, sometimes coming close together and again moving away to gain some space. Occasionally, they may find themselves far apart, but that does not mean the dance is over. If they are patient and do not bolt, they can draw close together again.[4]

What insights did you gain? Write them in the margin.

Timing is Everything

In talking about sex, choose your times and places the way porcupines make love—very carefully!

First of all, do not offer "constructive criticism" or express great displeasure immediately after your sexual experience. That's when your mate is the most vulnerable. Instead, use those intimate moments to bless each other. Even if there's an aspect that needs improvement, say something like, "I'm so glad you are my lover." Or, "I want no one else but you, forever."

At that moment, just after lovemaking, you have the incredible power to bless or to curse (and wound your mate's self esteem). Choose to bless at that moment; save the "improvement talk" for the next day.

When you talk, begin by telling your mate what you like. Talk about what you do well together. Be genuine. For some, it may take some forethought and preparation to articulate what you like about your sexual experiences. It's important to win each other's trust as you delve into this highly personal and sensitive part of your marriage.

Again, the XYZ formula is a great tool for communicating your feelings in a sensitive manner. Remember, you're talking to your lifelong partner about an incredibly sensitive area of your life together. Tread softly, but tread. Like sex itself, talking takes a little work, but it's worth the effort.

Underline words you feel are necessary for you and your spouse to get to the intimacy level you desire.

trusting	risking	sharing
adjusting	planning	experimenting

How about reading this to your mate?

> *Come, my love,*
>
> *let's go to the field;*
>
> *let's spend the night*
>
>> *among the henna blossoms.*
>
> *Let's go early to the vineyards;*
>
> *let's see if the vine has budded,*
>
> *if the blossom has opened,*
>
> *if the pomegranates are in bloom.*
>
> *There I will give you my love.*
>
> *The mandrakes give off a fragrance,*
>
> *and at our doors is every delicacy—*
>
> *new as well as old.*
>
> *I have treasured them up for you,*
>
>> *my love.*
>
> Song of Songs 7:11-13

DREAM TIME

Okay, this is the area where you can really dream! Guys, this is your big chance to share your preferences. Check some of the ideas below and/or add your own on the next page.

In our sex life together, here are some of my dreams:

____ Plan and complete an out-of-town romantic getaway (with lots of time for sex!).

____ Hold each other a lot more—perfect the art of "cuddling."

____ Take turns setting the mood for physical intimacy (a relaxing bath, music, candles, a new negligee, etc.).

____ Vary the room of the house or place for lovemaking.

____ Talk about how our sex life is going.

____ Hold hands in public.

____ Sit by me on the couch when we watch television.

____ Travel to every state in the union, spend the night, and make love in each of those wonderful states. (Are there only 50?)

____ Ask each other: "How can I be a better lover to you?"

____ Budget my energy to give myself physically to you.

____ Work on my self-image. My mate chose me, not someone else I think is beautiful or handsome.

We've given extra space for this assignment. Continue to express your creativity, because no two couples are going to envision the same experiences. This is your personal workbook, so put your thoughts down on paper, even if they may sound silly or extravagant.

— _____

— _____

— _____

— _____

— _____

— _____

— _____

At the next group session, you will share with your mate why you checked what you did , as well as your creative ideas. (Remember, there are no wrong answers here, as long as you're honest!)

The LORD God said, "It is not good for the man to be alone. I will make a helper for him…. This is why a man leaves his father and mother and bonds with his wife, and they become one flesh."
Genesis 2:18, 24

Our culture is so confused about sexual intimacy. Even as this book is being published, the nation is debating the definition of marriage. This week's study may be the most relevant of all. Don't miss the main point: Sexual intimacy can only be found in knowing God. When God brings two of His children together in marriage, and the two become one, the experience is extraordinary.

Our marriages are a powerful union, a powerful expression of the awesomeness of our God. Our culture hungers to know God. Let your marriage cry out: the answer is Jesus Christ.

An extraordinary sexual relationship is part of the abundant life God desires for you and your mate.

God created marriage and physical intimacy. It was His idea. God is on your side on this one. He wants your sex life to be extraordinary, just like the rest of your marriage! An extraordinary sexual relationship is part of the abundant life God desires for you and your mate. But getting to that level will take some work. Why not begin today?

---

[1] Dr. Kevin Leman, *Sheet Music: Uncovering the Secrets of Sexual Intimacy in Marriage* (Wheaton: Tyndale, 2003), back cover.
[2] Dr. Les Parrott III and Dr. Leslie Parrott, *Saving Your Marriage Before It Starts: Seven Questions to Ask Before (and After) You Marry* (Grand Rapids: Zondervan, 1995), 123.
[3] For a more thorough discussion on the XZY Formula, see the Parrott's book *Saving Your Marriage*.
[4] Alan Loy McGinnis, *The Romance Factor* quoted from *601 Quotes about Marriage and Family* by William and Nancie Carmichael (Wheaton: Tyndale, 1998), 32.

Extraordinary Marriage Plan Worksheet

	30 DAYS ACTION PLANS	60 DAYS ACTION PLAN	90 DAYS ACTION PLAN
3. Physical Intimacy			

Are You Wearing Emotional Masks?

Take the risk. Reveal the real you.

Each of you must put off falsehood and speak truthfully to his neighbor, for we are all members of one body.
Ephesians 4:25, NIV

In January of 1993 I (Selma) knew Mom was dying of breast cancer, but Dad refused to accept it. I'm a Daddy's girl, and to see him gripped by denial was heart wrenching. He was trying so hard to be the provider and protector that he had always been. But he could not protect Mom from death.

I'll never forget the night Dad finally broke. He came in from working the fields of his farm, sat down in "his" chair, and wept. I knelt beside him, held his hand, and cried too. Then Dad said something I'll always remember: "I have gone through everything with your Mom, but she's going someplace I can't go yet, and I want to go with her."

That's the example of emotional intimacy I witnessed in my parents' marriage. I really think Mom wouldn't let go until she knew Dad was willing to let her go. Two short weeks later, after 46 years of marriage, she left his arms, dying peacefully in her sleep. We all took great comfort in knowing that the second she left my Dad's warm and protective embrace, Jesus wrapped His arms around her.

That year was one of the most difficult journeys of my life, but along the way God gave me many gifts; one was Rodney. We had been married 16 years, and our commitment had never been more tested. During the year prior to Mom's death, I gave my all emotionally, physically, and spiritually to my parents. I traveled often from our home near Nashville to their farm in East Tennessee. It broke my heart every time I left Rodney and my two beautiful girls, ages nine and seven, standing on our front porch, waving good-bye.

Rodney was my anchor during that difficult time. You see, in giving so much to Mom and Dad, I had little left to give him. I would return home empty, exhausted, totally depleted. But rather than demanding I give to him, Rodney gave to me. He would lovingly wrap his arms around me, emotionally, physically, and spiritually renewing my strength. When I was too exhausted to pray, the Holy Spirit and my partner on the journey of life would intercede for me. Rodney stood in the gap, and gave me the freedom to feel and express every emotion churning inside me: anger, fear, guilt, and exhaustion. Never once did he say, "You shouldn't feel that way." Instead, he listened, and he allowed me the solace of silence.

Rodney stood in the gap, and gave me the freedom to feel and express every emotion churning inside me.

Rodney also became both Mom and Dad to Jennifer and Natalie during that time. I felt so much guilt about that, and Rodney would do everything he could to take away that guilt. He told me often in words and deeds, "I understand that you need to go and give to your Mom at this time." I needed to hear the word "go" because I so wanted to stay.

But that year one of the greatest things Rodney gave me was the gift of "no regrets." I have been able to redeem the time I lost with Rodney and the girls, but I could never do that with Mom. I had so many special moments with her during that year, powerful moments that have made me a better mom,

Slowly, awkwardly, with tears streaming down our faces, we reluctantly reached out to one another. Neither of us knew how much strength we had to give, but we were willing to share it. We gave one another something that most friendships are not able to give—vulnerability. Throughout our years together, we had built up a history and a closeness so subtle even we didn't know it was there. On that evening, we admitted we couldn't handle life alone. We needed one another.[2]
Erma Bombeck
A Marriage Made in Heaven or Too Tired for an Affair

a better wife, and a better person. When I came out of the fog of exhaustion (it took almost a year), Rodney was waiting patiently for me with his arms around our two precious daughters. I smile now just thinking about it.

In *One Flame*, Gary Smalley says, "Oneness is the strength of marriage, a safe harbor. It is the place where the couple is stronger than either partner is separately."[1]

Write about a time when you "stood in the gap" for your spouse—a time you met his/her emotional needs.

_____

_____

_____

Write about a time when your spouse "stood in the gap" for you.

_____

_____

_____

Rodney has seen me open and vulnerable. He has witnessed my good days and my bad—and he has loved me unconditionally through them all. Although that year was one of the most painful of my entire life, it built our marriage more than any other. You see, just as Genesis 2:25 describes, I stood before Rodney emotionally naked—and felt no shame.

Not long ago I shared with Rodney my fear of getting breast cancer. Rodney gave me assurance that he would be there with me every step of the way, whatever happened. It was a sobering conversation for both of us. Yet, there was depth. There was closeness. There was reality. There was emotional connection. We didn't wear masks. We didn't pretend. And that took our marriage to a new level of intimacy.

Underline the emotion(s) you can easily share with your spouse. Circle any that are more difficult to share.

anger   love   loneliness   embarrassment

joy   fear   insecurity   grief

trust   worry   compassion   disappointment

Wired by the Creator

To be connected emotionally is to take the risk of removing your masks and allowing your partner for life to see the real you. No concealing. No competition. Quite the contrary: you share your lives as teammates, cooperating, encouraging, and helping each other through this journey. You offer each other the treasures of peace, comfort, and the freedom to be yourself. What extraordinary gifts!

Read 2 Corinthians 1:3-4 in the margin.
- Underline the ultimate source of our comfort.
- Draw a box around the reason God comforts us.
- Put a wavy line under problems that God comforts.
- When your spouse needs comforting, circle whom you should look to for help.

We are to connect with our spouse the same way God connects with us. The more emotionally intimate we are with our spouses, the more we will be able to extend peace and comfort when they need it.

Blessed be the God and Father of our Lord Jesus Christ, the Father of mercies and and the God of all comfort. He comforts us in all our affliction, so that we may be able to comfort those who are in any kind of affliction, through the comfort we ourselves receive from God.
2 Corinthians 1:3-4

Don't you long for that? Don't you yearn to be connected to your spouse, for him or her to know you deeply—the real you—in every area of your life? God wired you to have that yearning. And He wove into your very DNA creativity, wisdom, love—and an incredible range of emotions to enable you and your mate to intimately experience life together.

In *The Christ of Easter,* Calvin Miller says, "Emotion is not the evidence that a religion is true, but emotion is always the by-product of true religion. Why? Everything which impacts our lives at the deepest level of our souls cannot help but elicit our deepest, most profound feelings."[3]

God feels the deepest of emotions, and He wants you to feel them too. As you learned in chapter two, God wants you to put Him first; He wants a deeply spiritual relationship with you. But He also wants to be intimate with you emotionally. Such emotional intimacy with God requires being real, making yourself vulnerable. You risk with God, and He loves it!

Read Psalm 34:17-18 in your Bible

What kind of person gets God's attention?

_____

To whom does the Lord stay near?

_____

Whom does He save (rescue)?

_____

I called to the Lord in my distress, and I cried to my God for help. From His temple He heard my voice, and my cry to Him reached His ears.
Psalm 18:6

God also wants you to be real with your mate. He created marriage as a safe haven for a man and woman to be vulnerable with one another. Begin today to take that risk with one another. Not only will God love it, you'll love it! God cannot do much with you or your spouse if you wear masks and play the game of surface relationships. But oh, the extraordinary things He can do when He has your hearts—your real unmasked hearts!

List some of the emotional masks people use to hide their real emotions. We've given you an example.

<u>**Happy Face**</u>   _____

_____   _____

_____   _____

Speaking of getting real, in the Psalms the deep and profound feelings of the writer are unmasked. A full range of heartfelt emotions is shared. In Psalm 61:1, the psalmist says, "God, hear my cry; pay attention to my prayer."

In your Bible, read the verses. Complete the chart to show the emotion expressed and the activity by which that emotion was expressed. We've given an example.

Scripture	Emotion	Activity
Psalm 95:1	Joy	Shouting
Psalm 100:2		
Psalm 102:1-2		
Psalm 130:5-6		

Just as the psalmist prayed for God to hear his cry, your ears need to be attentive to the cry of your spouse, to your mate's emotional voice. Have you been listening?

When you and your mate experience emotional intimacy, you will know your mate like no one else does. There's a certain extraordinary mystique about that. You are in an exclusive two-member club—just as God planned from the beginning.

Think about the intimate ways you know your spouse. Stop now to pray, thanking God for your spouse's strengths—especially those that only you know well! You may want to write these strengths as you pray.

Strengths:

_____

_____

_____

Erecting Guardrails

Giving yourselves to each other emotionally is not just a good idea; it's your responsibility. God wired you for emotional bonding, and the need is very powerful. When deprived of this type of intimacy, the enemy can tempt you. Read I Peter 5:8 in the margin. Often, he tries sending someone into your path who gives you the emotional attention that you crave from your mate. Then, in your mind, "the other man" or "the other woman" can quickly become everything you feel your mate is not. And that's a dangerous scenario.

Emotional bonding with someone else can easily slip into a physical relationship. Numerous couples have sat before me

Be sober! Be on the alert! Your adversary the Devil is prowling around like a roaring lion, looking for anyone he can devour.
1 Peter 5:8

(Rodney) seeking help from an affair begun by a lack of emotional connection within their marriage.

Christy came to me ready to leave her husband and three small children. She was "in love" with a coworker who wore suits, smelled good, and listened to her. They had emotionally connected. He really showed a desire to "know" Christy, and seemed to care about her feelings. Their work conversations expanded to sharing life together via email, then on the cell phone. In Christy's mind and heart, she gave herself to another man.

A woman shared with Selma that she had been emotionally involved with her Sunday school teacher for over three years. It almost destroyed her marriage. The irony? Her Sunday School teacher wasn't even aware of it! The "unfaithfulness" was taking place in this woman's mind. She asked God to forgive her and asked Selma to warn women of the dangers of emotional intimacy with anyone other than their spouses.

Read the following verses in your Bible. Each one shows two "mind-sets"—a mind that is set on the things of God and a mind that is set on fleshly, worldly thinking. Complete the sentences.

Romans 8:6
- The mind set on the flesh leads to _____.

- The mind set on God's Spirit leads to _____.

Romans 12:2
- We are not to conform our thinking to _____.

- We are to be transformed (changed) by the renewing of

  our _____.

Titus 1:15-16

- Those with pure hearts see what is _____.

- Those with defiled hearts see nothing as _____.

- Some who are defiled profess God with their _____,

    but deny Him with their _____.

Let's look at two critical guardrails to put in place.

1. *Guard your heart.*
   You should only think of one man/woman as your emotional home and that person is your mate. Connect fully with the wisdom, power, and protection provided in Philippians 4:7: "And the peace of God, which surpasses every thought, will guard your hearts and your minds in Christ Jesus." This protection and peace comes when you let your love for your spouse flow out of your love for God.

By seeking after Him, the by-product of peace will come. And it is that by-product of peace that will guard your heart, keeping it focused only on your mate.

Read these verses. Write the responsibility we bear in focusing on our mates.

1. 1 Corinthians 6:13,18 _____

2. 1 Corinthians 7:3-5 _____

3. 2 Corinthians. 7:1 _____

4. 1 Thessalonians. 4:3-4 _____

2. Don't share deeply with someone of the opposite sex.
Guard your emotions and share them only with God, your spouse, a Christian counselor, or a close friend of the same sex. Emotions are the subtlest of attractions. Physical attractiveness is easy to spot—and thus guard against. But a warm, caring, sensitive personality can draw you in so subtly, so smoothly, and so quickly, that if guardrails are not securely in place, you'll find yourself much closer to the cliff of emotional bonding than it is safe or wise to be.

If you're thinking, *That would never happen to me! I would never have an affair!* think again. Never overestimate yourself, and never underestimate the enemy.

There's a reason the Department of Transportation erects guardrails at dangerous curves in the road: without them, people would accidentally, but quickly, tumble over the edge.

It's not any different with our emotions. Boundaries must be established when relating to the opposite sex, or you can easily and quickly find yourself going over the edge emotionally.

The Bible gives reasons why God establishes boundaries in sexual relationships. Read this passage from 1 Corinthians 6:18-20. Underline the reasons.

> *Flee from sexual immorality! "Every sin a person can commit is outside the body," but the person who is sexually immoral sins against his own body. Do you not know that your body is a sanctuary of the Holy Spirit who is in you, whom you have from God? You are not your own, for you were bought at a price; therefore glorify God in your body.*

Never overestimate yourself, and never underestimate the enemy.

Complete these statements about what you just read.

- Sexual immorality defiles our _____.

- When we defile our bodies, we also defile the

  _____ who resides within us.

- We are not our own; our bodies and our souls were

  purchased at a very high _____.

- The price of our salvation is _____.

- What we do with our bodies either _____ God or dishonors Him.

For you to enjoy abundant emotional intimacy with your spouse, these guardrails must be in place at all times. Be alert constantly to the enemy's strategy to catch you off guard.

The Bible is very clear about the blessings and the problems of sexual desire. King David is often used as the poster boy for lust. His affair with Bathsheba resulted in a murder and the death of their son. David's example was not lost on his children. You may remember the story of David's daughter Tamar who was raped by her own stepbrother Amnon (2 Sam. 13). This sin also resulted in murder and estrangement by David's son Absalom, who fled to a neighboring country.

Eventually, Absalom tried to take over his father's kingdom and was killed in the process. Although God forgave David (see Ps. 51), he was not spared the consequences of his own action. We can choose sin; we cannot choose the results.

For you to enjoy abundant emotional intimacy with your spouse, these guardrails must be in place at all times.

Without guardrails, mates can become jealous, possessive, and suspicious. Who wouldn't be if their emotions were up for grabs every day? With God's boundaries in place you are free to enjoy a level of emotional intimacy that results in an extraordinary marriage!

Start Here
Ready or not, here's the BAM! question for this week. How would you describe your emotional intimacy with your spouse right now? On page 82 you will respond to an Emotional Intimacy Assessment.

During *Couple Talk* at your next group session you will share with your mate in general terms your assessment of your emotional intimacy. Remember, this is a time to grow and should not be a time to be critical.

After your talk, come back to this paragraph. Evaluate your experience. Answer Y (yes) or N (no).

____ Did you find that you and your mate share emotions fairly well?

____ Do you have some work to do before getting to a comfortable level of emotional intimacy?

____ Do you have LOTS of work to do? It doesn't matter. The fact that you responded is what matters.

Emotional oneness requires communication, and that's what you did. So congratulations on discovering where you are with each other! The improvements can begin later, but for now, you know your starting point. Be attentive and alert to when your mate is ready to break through the surface with you. The emotional connection is essential and well worth the effort! Now complete the assessment on page 82.

Emotional Intimacy Assessment

Circle the responses below that best fit.

1. My spouse and I are open about emotional issues.

   never   seldom   often   always

2. We share our feelings with each other.

   never   seldom   often   always

3. We ask each other, "What are you feeling?"

   never   seldom   often   always

4. I am in touch with how my mate is feeling.

   never   seldom   often   always

5. My mate is in touch with how I'm feeling.

   never   seldom   often   always

4. We give each other permission to express emotions.

   never   seldom   often   always

7. My mate knows me deeply, beyond the surface, and accepts who I am.

   never   seldom   often   always

8. I feel I know my mate deeply, beyond the surface, and accept him/her.

never   seldom   often   always

9. My mate encourages me.

never   seldom   often   always

10. I encourage my mate.

never   seldom   often   always

Diving Below the Surface
All of us have room for improving our emotional intimacy
with our mates. To move in the right emotional direction,
let's talk about talking.

Years ago, David and Vera Mace, a Quaker couple known as
the founders of the marriage enrichment movement in the
United States, taught Selma and me four levels of communication between mates.

As you read each level, write an example in the margin.
1. Stern Talk—Sarcastic, manipulative talk. The style with
   the stinger in its tail!

2. Surface Talk—Small talk: "Have you paid the electric bill
   this month?"

3. Search Talk—The dreaming stage when you share what
   your goals and ambitions are. (This should be much easier
   now because you have been dreaming together in the previous sessions.)

4. Straight Talk—The deepest level. At this level, whether
   the emotions are positive or negative, the mate feels freedom and safety to share them.

**There are four levels
of communication
between mates.**

Using these definitions, what percent of a typical day's conversation with your spouse takes place at each level of communication? List the percents in the blanks beside each.

___Stern Talk   ___Surface Talk

___Search Talk   ___Straight Talk

Selma and I like to draw a line between levels of Surface and Search talk. That line represents the difference between a couple merely sharing a house and one sharing a life together. To get beyond routine—yet often necessary—small talk, you need to take a major step.

It's much like walking up to a lake and sticking your toe in the water. What you sense when you do determines whether you'll go farther into the water. If the water is warm, if it's "receptive," it makes you want to go deeper. On the other hand, if it's cold, you'll pull your toe out quickly and stay right where you are.

When your mate shares even a little below the emotional surface, your response can determine where the conversation will go. If you're supportive, you're inviting him/her to go deeper and share more with you. If, however, you are critical or make fun of his/her dream or feeling, you're telling your mate that the water is cold; don't go any deeper.

A few years ago I shared with Selma one of my dreams (that's the Search Talk level). I told her I had always wanted to go deer hunting. (A quick note to animal rights people: deer are still safe from me!) Selma had two choices of how to respond. She could have laughed at me and said, "You've never been hunting before. You've never even shot a gun. You don't know anyone who hunts. You'll probably shoot yourself before you get settled in the blind!"

How do you think I would have responded if she had said that? Would I have risked sharing another dream with her? "Well, here's another dream, honey. What do you think of this one?" Nope. I would have retreated back to small talk where there was no risk—toe completely out of the water.

Here's how Selma actually responded. After she got over her surprise, she found a couple in our church, David and Scarlet, who own a farm and love to deer hunt. They invited us to their home for dinner, and I came away with a deer hunting video and a couple of copies of *White Tail* magazine.

David first took me practice shooting, and then later we went hunting. I saw a deer at 6:45 a.m., but it was too far away. Never saw another deer the rest of the day but had the time of my life. It was a dream fulfilled—not to kill a deer, but to go hunting!

In the blanks write an (I) for an inviting attitude or a (C) for a closed attitude.

_____ "You shouldn't feel that way!"
_____ "Help me understand what you're saying."
_____ "What can I do to help?"
_____ "I wouldn't do that if I were you."
_____ "I really don't want to talk about that."
_____ "Oh, that's just your imagination—don't worry."
_____ "I can understand why you feel that way."
_____ "Lot's of people have it worse than you."
_____ "Let's work on this issue together."

Selma's response greatly impacted my freedom to live out a life-long deer hunting dream. She made the water warm, inviting me to go deeper. Be aware of the influence you have with your mate when he/she wants to share emotionally with you. Encourage your mate to go deeper by asking him/her to elaborate on the dream or feeling.

Small Steps
If sharing feelings is not normally part of your marriage, take some small steps to open up with each other.

1. Start with the simple things. Try some of the following jump start questions.

   • One thing I have always wanted us to do is

   _____

   • If I could live anywhere else in the world, it would be

   _____.

   • If money were not an issue, I would like to

   _____.

   • I wish we had more time for _____.

   • One thing I need more from you is _____

   • To me, our future is _____

   • I feel afraid when _____

   • I feel loved when _____

2. Intentionally set aside time to focus on really talking with each other.

Given the fast pace of our lives today, it probably won't happen if it's not on the calendar! If you have small kids, for example, a dessert date on the living room floor (after the kids are asleep) works well. The idea is to get used to spending exclusive time with each other.

You may want to establish the ground rule that you can't talk about kids or work but just about yourselves, your ideas, dreams, goals, and feelings. This allows each of you to get in touch with the "you" beyond your individual roles.

3. If your mate shares a personal feeling with you, encourage him/her to "go deeper."

A good reflective response can open the door for more sharing. For example, let's say your husband/wife comes in from work one evening and says that the boss took credit for work your spouse did. You can say something reflective like, "Wow, you must be very hurt about that." With that response, you've made the water warm. Your mate can either go deeper or let it go. But he or she knows that 1) you haven't judged the feelings that were shown, and 2) you are willing to explore that deeper if he/she wishes.

Try asking a below-the-surface-question on a daily basis. Rather than "How was your day?"—often followed by "fine"—tune in to your spouse for an emotional read. "Honey, you seem tired (or angry, or depressed); how can I help? If now is not the time, talk about the day later. This allows you to stay connected emotionally.

A dessert date on the living room floor (after the kids are asleep) works well.

DREAM TIME

It's time to dream big! Check some of the ideas below and/or add your own in the margin. (Remember, there are no wrong choices here. Just be honest!)

Here are some emotional dreams for my marriage:
___ I'd like for us to do a daily feelings check, asking each other at the end of the day "How do you feel?"
___ I want us to share quality "good-byes" in the mornings and "hellos" when we reunite in the evenings.
___ I want to become a student of my mate, to discover and meet his/her unique needs.
___ I want to strive to "risk" with my mate, getting below the surface of communication, getting to the deeper level of who I am and who my mate is.
___ I want to encourage and affirm my mate to reach his/her full potential.
___ I want to budget my energy to have the reserves to give emotionally to my mate.
___ I want to go on regular dates with my spouse to give us time to remove our masks.
___ I want my spouse and I to learn to play together; playfulness can lead to emotional openness.
___ I want to take the initiative and ask, "Honey, you seem to be distracted (or sad, upset, happy, angry). Can we share this together by talking about it?"

---

[1]Gary Smalley, *One Flame* (Wheaton, IL: Tyndale House, 2002), 3.
[2]Erma Bombeck, *A Marriage Made in Heaven or Too Tired for an Affair* quoted from *601 Quotes about Marriage and Family* by William and Nancie Carmichael (Wheaton: Tyndale, 1998), 36.
[3]Calvin Miller, *The Christ of Easter: Readings for the Season of Resurrection* (Nashville: Broadman and Holman, 2004), 6.

Extraordinary Marriage Plan Worksheet

	30 DAYS ACTION PLANS	60 DAYS ACTION PLAN	90 DAYS ACTION PLAN
4. Emotional Intimacy			

Week Five

Do You Know Your Dragons?

Slaying the enemies to an extraordinary marriage

To Him who is able to do above and beyond all that we ask or think— according to the power that works in you.
Ephesians 3:20, NIV

**Back then Selma and I were both stuffers, and absolutely clueless about how to handle conflict.
--Rodney**

Early in our marriage Selma and I discovered we had a dragon living with us. He was a nasty, fire-breathing beast, bent on keeping us far away from each other— and certainly a great distance from an extraordinary marriage. The beast was the two-headed dragon of unresolved conflict and unforgiveness.

Back then, Selma and I were both stuffers, and absolutely clueless about how to handle conflict. Whenever we had a disagreement, I would emotionally withdraw from Selma, and she would physically retreat from me, which was no small feat in our tiny two-room apartment!

Even when the smoke of a disagreement would clear, and we would move back together physically, there was always a little more distance in our relationship because we never dealt with the conflict or asked each other's forgiveness. Our two-headed beast was going the distance to ensure that Selma and I kept our distance from each other.

I thank God that He sent dragon slayers David and Vera Mace to teach Selma and me the danger of this very real

90

enemy of our relationship. You'll recall from week 4 that the Maces are credited for beginning the marriage enrichment movement. This couple taught us how to deal with the dragons of conflict and unforgiveness so we could clear the air, give and receive forgiveness, have a deeper level of intimacy, and embrace the potential for our marriage. This week, we'll share some of the wisdom we learned from David and Vera, who gave us our first glimpse of a truly extraordinary relationship.

By this point in the study, Selma and I pray that you and your mate are dreaming together, that you see your potential to build or extend the foundation of your own relationship. But we must warn you: Dragons live in your home too. Dragons can keep you distanced from each other and imprisoned in the land of ordinary. Dragons that—when not dealt with properly—can singe the very fabric of your marriage, or worse yet, leave it in ashes.

Selma and I have had several other dragons reside in our home over the years—nasty, smelly creatures who absolutely refused to leave until we joined forces and proactively kicked them out! Every now and then, we'll spot them sulking on the fringes of our relationship, just waiting for a point of reentry; dragons are very predatory. Tolkien had it right when he cautioned, "It does not do to leave a dragon out of your calculations, if you live near him."[1]

You and your spouse must be battle ready. Don't ignore, avoid, try to go around, under, or over the dragons. Attack them. Determine, individually and together, that nothing is going to keep you from experiencing what God planned for your marriage. No dragon is going to keep you apart spiritually, physically, or emotionally. Set your vision, dream your dreams, and as 1 Timothy 6:12 exhorts: "Fight the good fight of the faith. Take hold of the eternal life to which you were called" (NIV).

Dragons—when not dealt with properly—can singe the very fabric of your marriage, or worse yet, leave it in ashes.

It does not do to leave a live dragon out of your calculations, if you live near him.[1]
J.R.R. Tolkien

91

Once you know who they are, you and your mate can throw them out.

Call Your Dragons by Name

Dragons impede intimacy with your spouse. To counter their attack, identify them. Once you know who they are, you and your mate can throw them out. Is it hard work? Absolutely. But the reward is great!

Circle the dragons that currently reside in your home. Add any not listed here.

What Dragons Live in Our House?

Busyness	Unforgiveness	Unresolved Conflict
Workaholism	Poor Self Esteem	Critical spirit
Boredom	Dishonesty	Laziness
Inappropriate Behavior		Inconsiderate behavior
Insensitivity	Lack of Trust	Debt
Parenting Issues		Step Parenting Issues
Extended Family Issues		Wounded Feelings
Health Issues	Infidelity	Abuse
Lack of Communication		Lying

_____

_____

_____

Who's Feeding Your Dragons?

Now that you have a good picture of the dragons that are wreaking havoc in your marriage, understand that these beasts are most often fed by Satan, selfishness, and the world.

1. *Satan Feeds Your Dragons.*

   His first assignment is to keep you out of God's Kingdom. He loses that battle when you accept Jesus Christ and follow Him. But then Satan goes to Plan "B," which is to keep you and your mate from experiencing an abundant life. And Satan is very adept at implementing Plan B!

Read the following verses in your Bible. Match each verse with the description of Satan's "Plan B."

a. John 10:10   ___ The enemy wants to exploit you with deception, getting you to follow unrestrained lifestyles.

b. 1 Timothy 6:9   ___ Satan sets a trap of temptation to bring you to ruin and destruction.

c. 2 Peter 2:1-3   ___ The thief [the enemy] comes only to steal, kill and destroy.

Fill in the blanks to find the antidote to his schemes.

2 Corinthians 4:2   Renounce secret and _____ things, don't use distortion or

_____, but openly put forth the truth.

Ephesians 6:11   Put on the full _____ of God so you can stand up against

the _____ of the Devil.

Don't ever underestimate the enemy's desire to destroy everything godly, including the sanctity of marriage.

Don't ever underestimate the enemy's desire to destroy everything godly, including the sanctity of marriage. He wants to defile your marriage.

How can we be on the outlook for him? God's Word warns in 1 Peter 5:8, "Be sober! Be on the alert! Your adversary the Devil is prowling around like a roaring lion, looking for anyone he can devour. Resist him, firm in the faith."

Resist the enemy—fight him with the truth of God's Word. Satan will tell you, "There's too much sin in your life. God can't help you. You've messed up again, and there's no hope for your marriage." But the truth of God's Word says, "If we confess our sins, He is faithful and righteous to forgive us our sins and to cleanse us from all unrighteousness" (I John 1:9).

2. *Selfishness Feeds Your Dragons.*
   Yikes! Now we're getting personal! This one stings a bit, doesn't it? But the meet-my-needs-first mentality regularly feeds all sorts of dragons from the trough of selfishnesss. Sadly, we have met the enemy, and he is us!

Look up these verses in your Bible and write in the blank the correct consequence of selfishness. Here are some clue words: dissatisfaction, isolation, strife, loss of integrity, suffering, disorder, and death.

Proverbs 18:1 _____

Galatians 5:19-21 _____

James 3:14-16 _____

Selfish people grow comfortable with selfish practices, isolating them from others and from the presence of God.

Read the verses in your Bible. Find how to defeat selfishness. Fill in the blank.

Luke 9:23   Christ says in order to have life we must

                _____ ourselves.

Philippians 2:3   We are to do nothing out of selfishness or

                conceit, but are to consider _____ as better or more important than ourselves.

Henry and Richard Blackaby remind us to "Resist the temptation to pursue your own goals and ask God to bless them. Rather, deny yourself and join the activity of God around you as He reveals it to you."[2]

How do you fight your selfish nature? Die daily to yourself and live for Christ! More than once I (Rodney) have encouraged a spouse to change jobs due to misplaced priorities. The spouse put his or her job, with the accolades it produced and the security it represented, ahead of the marriage. Each time a spouse has recognized the selfishness of misplaced priorities and changed employment to overcome it, God has (with a lot of hard work on the couples' part) restored the marriage.

That's living with an attitude of "I'm going to honor God by putting my marriage before my comfort zone of job security." God honors that commitment. Ephesians 5:25 says that we husbands are to love our brides as Christ loved the church (His bride) and gave Himself up for her. Such an attitude will kill any selfishness in your marriage.

Any of us can succumb to this threat. Mothers may put their children ahead of their spouses. Husbands may put sports in

"I'm going to honor God by putting my marriage before my comfort zone."

first place ahead of their marriages. The biggest danger of all is putting anything before our intimacy with God.

3. *The World Feeds Your Dragons.*

Everyday you are bombarded by the messages from an ungodly world, and if you are not aware of its power, the dragons that are fed by cultural seduction become even more powerful. When preparing to battle your dragons, these verses can help you stand strong against the world's forces that feed them.

Read these verses in your Bible. Fill in the blanks.

1 Corinthians 2:12-16   God, through His Spirit, will make spiritual things known to believers, helping us to discern with the mind

of _____.

Colossians 2:8-9   The world offers only empty

_____, but those in Christ

have been _____ by Him.

Jesus spoke of the world in Matthew 13:22, "The worries of this age and the seduction of wealth choke the word, and it becomes unfruitful". If you will allow our paraphrase: The world keeps you from experiencing an extraordinary life and marriage! How do you fight the world? "The One who is in you is greater than the one who is in the world" (1 John 4:4).

"Worldly wisdom" says that money is the highest value. You've probably heard the quip, "We buy things we don't need, with money we don't have, to impress people we don't like." As you try to meet everyone else's expectations of you, the pull of the world can rob joy from your relationship. Matthew 6:31 essentially says, "Don't go there! Don't get caught up in such unimportant things. Rely on the Lord." (author's paraphrase).

Evict Your Dragons

Selma and I could write an entire book on dragons, but we've chosen to focus on the four we most often confront in our marriage ministry. Our goal is to help you proactively deal with the most common dragons to deepen the level of intimacy and embrace the potential of an extraordinary marriage.

1. The Busyness Dragon

Now are you ready for the biggest fire-breather of them all? Listen to the eviction notice. "Be still, and know that I am God" (Psalms 46:10, NIV). We can often get caught up in thinking that activity is equivalent to productivity—that success is defined as "doing more."

"Be still."

We don't hear that phrase very often in our twenty-first century world—unless we're saying it to our kids in the back seat! In our desire to be the best husband, wife, parent, employee, minister, Sunday school teacher, room mother, (you fill in the blank) we give power to the busyness dragon.

I (Selma) once heard someone say that **BUSY** means
    Being
    Under
    Satan's
    Yoke
Well, look around. Lots of married couples certainly look like they're under a heavy yoke. They're absolutely exhausted. Are you and your spouse among this worn-out crowd?

> We can often get caught up in thinking that activity is equivalent to productivity—that success is defined as "doing more."

It's all too easy to forget where you are going—and why—when you're in perpetual motion!

In the rat race of life, extraordinary marriages can seem more like a myth than a God-created reality. Remember that telling quote from week 1? "And he mounted his horse and rode off in all directions ..." If your daily pattern is to grab a quick kiss as you gallop by your spouse in the morning, and another before you tumble off your horse onto your pillow at night, it's time to say, "Whoa!" It's all too easy to forget where you are going—and why—when you're in perpetual motion!

For this "busyness checkup," check *yes* **or** *no.*

Yes	No	
____	____	1. I frequently miss reading the Bible because of my busy schedule.
____	____	2. I usually feel exhausted by day's end.
____	____	3. I lack time to even look at my "to do" list.
____	____	4. I get frustrated trying to prioritize the tasks that need to be accomplished.
____	____	5. I rarely have quiet, alone time just for me.
____	____	6. I experience anxiety over all the demands on my time.
____	____	7. I'm gone from home more evenings of the week than I am at home.
____	____	8. A weekend get-away is usually impossible.
____	____	9. I have trouble sleeping at night because I'm thinking of what I need to get done.
____	____	10. When I'm accomplishing one task, I'm already thinking of the next one.
____	____	Total the number of *yes* and *no* responses.

If you had 7-10 *yes* responses, you are being burned up by the busyness dragon. If you had 4-6 *yes* responses, he's breathing his fire down your back. If you had 0-3, some armor is in place, but watch any places you checked for weak spots!

The busyness dragon's daily mantra is "Keep 'em moving so they won't realize what they're missing." Married couples can easily become involved in so many arenas—individually and as a twosome or family—that they have no time for sharing life intimately with God or each other. You can't know God unless you stop galloping in all directions and, in stillness, spend intimate time with Him, talking, sharing, reading His love letter (the Bible), and just plain old listening.

The same is true of marriage. Be still and know each other: talk, share God's love-letter together, and just plain old listen to each other. A commitment to stillness spells doom for the busyness dragon. Read the comforting words of Jesus in Matthew 11:28-30 (margin).

Now let's examine these suggestions for slaying dragon #1.

1. *Establish "Our Night."*
   Get out your calendar and "schedule" some non-busyness time each week. Keep the television and the computer turned off, and seek to re-schedule any meetings. Tell your mate that you want to get off the world's merry-go-round and spend some time getting to know each other again. That will be music to your mate's ears.

Don't know what to talk about? Initially choose safe topics and those that cannot be answered with a simple yes or no, such as What is your ideal vacation spot? Who was your best teacher? Between the ages of 8-10, what did you want to be when you grew up? And so on.

Because everyone's schedule is packed, your first date might need to be scheduled a few weeks from now. That's okay; schedule it anyway. The fact that you spend time with each other on a consistent basis is the point. Don't panic if you

Come to Me, all you who are weary and burdened, and I will give you rest. All of you, take up My yoke and learn from Me, because I am gentle and humble in heart, and you will find rest for yourselves. For My yoke is easy and My burden is light.
Matt. 11:28-30

miss a night. Jump right back in the next week. Some events involving others we can't change. Remember my (Selma's) experience during the last months of my mother's life (week 2)? There are seasons in every life you can't control.

Perhaps child-rearing has become your—pardon the word—excuse for lack of couple time. Even parents of preschoolers can schedule time with each other after the kids are put to bed. Parents can use that time cleaning the kitchen, working in the garage, or paying bills. Don't give even high priority items time taken from your commitment to being friends and lovers. Your children will bless you later.

2. *Overhaul our family's schedule..*
   An overscheduled family will likely be overtaken by the big guy with the fiery nostrils. How can we stop him? Limit your kid's sports involvement to one sport. Embrace one ministry as a couple instead of always serving individually. Don't accept roles chosen for you by others.

Write your answers to these questions in the margin.
How many weekly evening activities do you typically have?
To how many ministries are you committed?
Can you prioritize your ministry involvement—top 2 or 3?
What other distractions will you eliminate or choose rarely?

Have you discovered the companionship of shared tasks? Work together to accomplish family chores (not I'll dust one room while you dust another, unless the saved minutes will give you private time together). You'd be surprised what you can talk about while chopping vegetables or pulling weeds.

Put your television in the attic for a few months. Don't answer the telephone during mealtimes. Establish a time limit for use of the computer.

In a sense, this entire book is designed to help you fight the dragon of busyness. With God's guidance, you and your mate can develop a proactive plan that gives you focus rather than allowing the chaos of life to control your time, your marriage, and your life. Keep priorities straight by choosing Bible study, prayer, and worship as a normal part of every week.

2. The Boredom Dragon

The life Jesus died to give us is anything but boring! An extraordinary marriage is a sense of adventure with God. Remember, we're on a marriage journey. Dreaming dreams and planning together provides a great offense against the boredom dragon (the subtlest of all beasts). He banks on the fact that couples often forget how to have fun and enjoy life! The boredom dragon can rob you of the joy of living by just keeping things routine day after day.

Dreaming dreams and planning together provides a great offense against the boredom dragon.

Answer the following BAM questions with real dates or descriptions.

1. When was the last time you and your spouse just "played" together? _____

2. When was the last time you and your spouse did something adventurous? _____

3. When was the last time you got out of your comfort zone to do ministry together?

_____

If you couldn't write a response to these questions, don't worry! There's no better time than right now to begin making memories. Start a new adventure. God designed us for adventure. When boredom sets in, that's a big danger sign! So is restlessness. And when restlessness takes root, we have often

Who better to ask for creativity than the Great Creator himself?

seen a husband or wife seek that adventure with someone other than their spouse. Instead, "Enjoy life with the wife you love" (Eccl. 9:9). If you feel a bit rusty in the fun department, ask God to open your eyes to show you how to spice up your life. In other words, pray for creativity! And who better to ask for creativity than the Great Creator himself? But once you make this request, buckle up! Your marriage will take off in areas you've never dreamed of.

Pause right now for prayer. You may want to write your prayer or just list key words, asking God to bring fresh creativity into your marriage.

My prayer:_____

_____

_____

_____

From time to time Selma reminds me that she likes surprises. It doesn't have to be big shockers, such as kidnapping her for a month-long getaway to Tahiti. (I've never tried that one. Thank goodness! She probably would love it!) Detouring from my daily routine to do something special for her keeps our relationship fresh. Simply bringing Selma a flower at the end of the day puts her smile in full bloom. And Selma is the ultimate re-enforcer.

It doesn't matter how small the gesture, she is so proud of what I've done. I respond to that positive reinforcement like Pavlov's dog when the bell rang! If Selma thinks I'm creative, no matter how small my effort might have been, it motivates me to do even more creative stuff for our marriage. Whatever

I do, I know Selma is going to appreciate and brag on it.
To keep the boredom dragon far from your door (or to toss
him out with style), seek to grow in these actions:

- Be grateful and affirming when your mate takes a step—
  even a baby step—in the direction of doing something to
  keep your marriage alive.
- Learn to play. Do something just for fun. Play tennis,
  watch a favorite old movie, or share an ice cream cone.
  Recall the early days of your marriage when buying an
  ice cream cone was a big splurge.
- Learn something new together. Try something you've
  never done before. Learn to water (or snow) ski. Tackle
  a new language. Trace your family tree.
- Develop a spontaneous muscle. When the sun is pouring
  through your windows on a Saturday, learn to seize the
  moment. Leave the laundry piled where it is and go stick
  your feet in a nearby creek, plant yourself on a blanket in
  a park, or just fly a kite. Playing refuels our tanks.

Don't get us wrong; we're not talking about throwing routine
out the door with the boredom dragon. Everyone in the family
would constantly be exasperated because of the disorganiza-
tion and stress, which is a dragon that has some real teeth in
lots of homes. And yet, overdoing routine is dangerous as well.
Ask God for wisdom to strike the balance needed between
stability and freshness in your marriage.

3. The Money Dragon
Talk about a dragon that can really drag your marriage down;
the money dragon is a greedy greenback with lots of muscle!
He can wreak havoc whether there's too little cash or too
much. Most married couples have locked heads over money.
So how do you oust the money dragon? Matthew 10:8
capsules it, "Freely you have received, freely give" (NIV).
Hoarding is as deadly as over-spending.

For the love of money is a root of all kinds of evil, and by craving it, some have wandered away from the faith and pierced themselves with many pains.
1 Timothy 6:10

God's word alerts us. Read 1 Timothy 6:10 (margin).

1. Circle the phrase that describes the root of evil.
2. Underline the direction our hearts go when we crave money.
3. Put a box around the final consequence—the end result.

Other ousting strategies are proven winners. Check any of the following you would like to implement.

❑ 1. Talk about money. You bring into your marriage how you were taught to view money and material things in your home. Maybe you were taught to save, and your mate was taught to charge. Get on the same page. (See the next idea.)

❑ 2. Establish a money plan. Agree on a budget, a debt reduction plan, and a savings plan. One of you should manage the details based on giftedness, but both of you must set up a regular time to review your plan.

❑ 3. Determine to be open and honest about money. Never hide money issues or lie about them. This spirit of concealing is a huge danger sign in a marriage.

❑ 4. Get help if you're stuck. There are many great Christian money guides available today. Financial counselors can help you get on the right track, which may include a plan to pay off all your debt. Christian book stores have several books on this subject. Or, ask other church members for the name of a qualified Christian with whom you can talk about money issues such as a banker or financial planner.

❑ 5. Budget your expenditures, including some "fun money" as a reward for your hard labor. Saving together can build a relationship. I (Selma) remember the time when Rodney and I would drop our loose change in a tennis can. When the can was full, we would count it and then plan a fun date. That was all the fun money we had! We celebrated cheap, but we had fun!

❏ 6. Set aside a percent of your money to give to the Lord. This is a biblical principle that honors God. He owns 100% of your money, just like He owns 100% of your lives. He wants you to join other believers in the joy of giving through your local church. Giving freely energizes your life and marriage. Follow the sage advice of martyred missionary Jim Elliot: "He is no fool who gives what he cannot keep to gain what he cannot lose." The money dragon can't survive by this biblical philosophy.

4. The Dragon of Unresolved Conflict
We've saved what may well be the most lethal enemies for last—the two-headed beast of unresolved conflict and unforgiveness. Remember our story about this dragon's grip on our marriage? (See pp. 90-91.) Here are some of the key principles we have learned from others.

As you read Ephesians 4:26-27 in the margin, underline the most important words.
1. Anger is not a sin.
2. Within 24 hours you should deal with your anger.
3. Resolving your anger prevents the conflict dragon from building a barrier in your marriage.

There are three ways to handle anger and conflict: Suppress it. Express it. Process it. Let me (Rodney) tell a story to illustrate. Let's say you and your spouse are going down the road, and your car's oil light comes on. You have three choices:

1. EXPRESS your feelings. You can take a hammer and smash the light. Problem fixed? No. Soon the engine of the car is going to lock up and there will be major problems.
2. SUPPRESS your feelings. You can ignore the oil light. Soon the engine locks up. (Selma and I were masters at this the first five years of our marriage.)

"Be angry and do not sin. Don't let the sun go down on your anger, and don't give the Devil an opportunity."
Ephesians 4:26-27

3. PROCESS your feelings. You can stop the car, get out, lift the hood and find the real problem.

The problem is not the oil light; that just indicates the problem. In marriage, the oil light represents anger. It indicates something underneath needs attention. As a couple, lift the hood of your marriage and together figure out what the problem is—and fix it. If you can't fix it, share the problem with your pastor, a Christian counselor, or an accountability group such as the group that is meeting together for this study.

May the words of my mouth and the meditation of my heart be acceptable to You, LORD, my rock and my Redeemer.
Psalm 19:14

Those who love to "get it off their chests" yell, say hurtful things, and often act out their anger. After the explosion, they feel great! Meanwhile, those in the wake of their expressions are picking up the pieces—emotionally recovering. Weeks may pass before the target of the verbal attack recovers from the results of unbridled expression!

Examine each of the verses. Underline the part that describes what the tongue can do. In the blank before each verse write (G) for good or (E) for evil.

___ Psalm 10:7—"Cursing, deceit, and violence fill his mouth; trouble and malice are under his tongue."
___ Psalm 35:28—"My tongue will proclaim Your righteousness, Your praise all day long."
___ Psalm 52:2—"Like a sharpened razor, your tongue devises destruction, working treachery."
___ Proverbs 15:4—"The tongue that heals is a tree of life."
___ James 3:6—"The tongue is a fire. The tongue, a world of unrighteousness, … it pollutes the whole body, sets the course of life on fire, and is set on fire by hell."

Suppressing anger (or stuffing it) is the most prevalent style chosen by couples. For Christians, it's quite frequently used because somewhere, deep down inside, resides the belief that it really is a sin to be angry and have conflict. WRONG. You can only stuff your emotional volcano so long before it erupts. Perhaps it will explode in an affair. Or we have seen it "quietly" explode with one person leaving his or her spouse for good. The other mate may be clueless that anything was wrong. Anyway you look at it, stuffing anger is unhealthy. Selma and I know. We were pros at it.

Are you a stuffer? Check any of these thoughts you have had.
☐ I just won't speak to him/her.
☐ I'm so mad I could explode, but saying something won't do any good.
☐ I'll just forget it. Maybe it will all blow over.
☐ There's no need to talk. We're beyond the talking stage.

If you checked any of these, it might be helpful to remember the Bible's admonition against "stuffing" in Zechariah 8:16: "These are the things you must do: Speak truth to one another; render honest and peaceful judgments in your gates."

Processing anger makes for an extraordinary marriage. That's when you talk together about the issue in question and come to some resolution. Sometimes you just say, "I'm sorry, will you forgive me?" Powerful words. Sometimes you need to compromise—meet in the middle on the issue. Sometimes you "agree to disagree" until you can resolve the issue at a later time. All of these lead to a healthy, growing relationship—and an evicted dragon.

Why does Ephesians say to deal with anger "before the sun goes down?" Because when you stuff your anger, conflict becomes even more serious: it results in resentment and bitterness. Some of the most difficult counseling I (Rodney)

For many, evicting the dragon of unresolved conflict is absolutely the hardest.

have done involves couples who have years of stuffed issues. They wake up one day full of resentment and bitterness and don't even know all the reasons why. Many couples find evicting the dragon of unresolved conflict absolutely the hardest because it adds a layer of tough scales every time a conflict is not resolved properly. Over time, couples find it harder to get to the heart of their problems.

To process conflict in a healthy way, follow these guidelines.
1. Get the anger out of the conflict before processing it. Cool down before you talk but commit to talk as soon as possible.
2. Stick to the issue and stay on the subject.
3. See yourself as a team. Always remember who the real enemy is; it's not you or your mate! Attack the problem, not the person
4. Affirm your spouse and your marriage during discussions.
5. Be responsible for your own anger. No one has made you angry. You chose to deal with the problem with anger.
6. Take the lead in resolving the issue. Your spouse may be clueless there is a problem.
7. Find a peacemaker if necessary.
8. Use "I" statements when telling your spouse you're angry. "I got angry when you made fun of me." Or, "I felt unimportant when you were late and didn't call."
9. Anger is often a secondary emotion triggered by jealousy, insecurity, fear, fatigue, or other feelings. Accept that feelings aren't right or wrong; they just are.
10. Forgive, forgive, and forgive. "I forgive you" may be the most under-utilized word in the English language.

Unforgiveness
The fire of this two-headed dragon of conflict and unforgiveness can gradually become so all-consuming and so oppressive that it can literally suck the air and life out of a home and a

marriage. Marriage allows us lots of room for unforgiveness to spread its wings because both spouses are going to make mistakes. If not properly handled, the resulting friction can cause more pain and hurt feelings.

Kent and Alissa sat in my (Rodney's) office. Alissa looked confused as to why they were there. Then, in tears, Kent told her of his affair. In a broken voice he said, "I've done this. I'm terribly sorry, and I desperately need you to forgive me." His plea for forgiveness was the first thing out of his mouth after sharing the painful news.

I explained to Kent that, although he desired forgiveness immediately, it might not come for a while. Alissa needed to let the shock of his betrayal sink in. My word to Alissa, in later sessions, was to be aware of the significance of forgiving Kent. If and when she extended forgiveness, it would not be the end of the issue, but it could be the beginning point of restoring their marriage.

Respond to these questions:
Is there something for which you need to seek forgiveness from your spouse? ❏ yes   ❏ no

Is there something for which you need to extend forgiveness to your spouse? ❏ yes   ❏ no

When will you take care of this? _____

Don't forget to repent before God for having a spirit of unforgiveness!

To date, Alissa has not verbally forgiven Kent. Although his adultery created an obvious barrier, the dragon of unforgiveness keeps the barrier between this couple heavily

If you forgive people their wrongdoing, your heavenly Father will forgive you as well. But if you don't forgive people, your Father will not forgive your wrongdoing.
Matthew 6:14-15

fortified. Alissa needs to move toward forgiveness at her own speed, but she should not park somewhere on the road. The price of unforgiveness is too high.

Read Matthew 6:14-15 in the margin. Underline the consequence of unforgiveness.

In his book, *When Forgiveness Doesn't Make Sense,* Robert Jeffress says, "The wounds of the past can never be changed. But they can be healed, and forgiveness is a procedure God has given us to accomplish that physical, emotional, and spiritual renewal in our lives."[3]

Asking for and granting forgiveness is not easy, but it is intimate. There are few things as open and honest as one soul confessing to another, "I've done you wrong and need your forgiveness. Will you give it to me?" Talk about being vulnerable and taking a risk! When you or your mate offer the forgiveness that's being sought, the payoff is enormous. Security and dignity are restored and trust has multiplied. You see, intimacy will grow in that moment because unforgiveness is a powerful dragon. But forgiveness is even more powerful.

After learning how to work through our anger, Selma and I went back and dealt with every unresolved issue we could remember. Then we began to apply these principles to any conflict we had in our current relationship, asking each other's forgiveness many times along the way.

A powerful thing began to happen. No longer could the enemy bring up issues from our past because we processed them when they occurred. There was no stockpile of anger, bitterness, or resentment for the dragon to feed on. We literally starved him to death!

What replaced the two-headed dragon was the freedom to let God's Spirit fill our lives. Galatians 5:22 says: "The fruit of the Spirit is love, joy, peace, patience, kindness, goodness, faith, gentleness, self control. Against such things there is no law." Now that's the mantra of an extraordinary marriage!

Conquered Dragons

As long as you and your spouse are living in this world, you are going to battle dragons. Use Galatians 5:22-23 and John 4:14 as your swords to chase dragons from your home. Be proactive! Don't allow anything to come between you and your relationship with your spouse. Be aggressive and intentional about keeping your home dragon free. That way, you can replace hot air with fresh air, breathe deeply, and draw extraordinarily close to your spouse.

As we close this week about dragons, pray this prayer with your spouse: "God protect us from Satan, from our own selfish natures, and from the pull of the world. Forgive us for allowing anything to keep us from experiencing the life and relationships you planned for us. We pray our marriage will be extraordinary for your honor and your glory."

Even after a rough day of battling dragons, with this prayer and a renewed commitment to your marriage, you and your spouse can valiantly repeat the words of the mighty warrior Vicomte Turenne: "The enemy came. He was beaten. I am tired. Goodnight."[4]

Whoever drinks from the water that I will give him will never get thirsty again–ever! In fact, the water I will give him will become a well of water springing up within him for eternal life.
John 4:14

[1]J.R.R. Tolkien, *BrainyQuote,* [cited 6 July 2004]. Available from the Internet: *www.hiplists.com.*
[2]Henry Blackaby and Richard Blackaby, *Experiencing God Day by Day Devotional* (Nashville: Broadman and Holman, 1998), 48.
[3]Robert Jeffress, *When Forgiveness Doesn't Make Sense* (Colorado Springs: Waterbrook Press, 2000), 167.
[4]Vicomte de Turenne, message sent after the battle of Dunes, 1658.

Dream Time

What dragons are keeping you from fulfilling some of the things you've been dreaming about in previous weeks? It's time to learn how to combat them. Be intentional. Don't let anything rob you of the abundant life Jesus came to give you!

Our Dragon Slaying Dreams

Check any of the dreams below that you would like to include in your marriage plan—or add your own.

___ Block off time in our schedule for us and for our family.

___ Review our schedule and say *no* to some things.

___ Get out of debt! Build a budget together.

___ Plan something fun together on a regular basis.

___ Take turns planning a date.

___ Commit to talk about issues, not to stuff them.

___ Learn to ask, "Will you forgive me?"

___ Learn to say, "I forgive you."

___ _____

___ _____

___ _____

___ _____

Extraordinary Marriage Plan Worksheet

	30 DAYS ACTION PLANS	60 DAYS ACTION PLAN	90 DAYS ACTION PLAN
5. Combating the Enemies			

Are You Ready for an Extraordinary Future?

Don't look back with regrets. Look forward to possibilities.

For I know the plans I have for you, declares the LORD, plans to prosper you and not to harm you, plans to give you hope and a future. Then you will call upon me and come and pray to me, and I will listen to you.
Jeremiah 29:11-12 (NIV)

As we come to the end of this study, Selma and I pray that in the previous weeks you and your spouse have dreamed together and now look forward to your future with great expectation and excitement! This week is designed to help you make your dreams come true. But the dream-come-true work is up to you. You need a high energy level. If you don't put some muscle behind it, it just won't happen.

When our girls were little, we dreamed of building them a tree house, but time and life kept slipping away. Now it's too late; Jennifer and Natalie are in college, building new dreams of their own. The tree house dream will forever go unfulfilled.

Some dreams left unfulfilled are more critical than others. What if you stopped now, at the dreaming stage of your marital planning? Does it really matter that you move beyond the dreams you've listed in each of the previous weeks to take steps to make those dreams come true? Does it really matter that your marriage moves from the chains of the past to the freedom of the future? Does it really matter that you move from the book of mistakes to the yet-to-be written pages of adventure and possibilities? Does it really matter that you leave an ordinary marriage behind and embrace an extraordinary one?

It certainly matters to God. But the choice is up to you. If you so choose, you can have an extraordinary marriage because you are loved and empowered by the grace of an extraordinary God. God's grace allows you to forget the past and press on toward the future. Paul says it well in Philippians 3:12-14.

> *Not that I have already reached [the goal] or am already fully mature, but I make every effort to take hold of it because I also have been taken hold of by Christ Jesus. Brothers, I do not consider myself to have taken hold of it. But one thing I do: forgetting what is behind and reaching forward to what is ahead, I pursue as my goal the prize promised by God's heavenly call in Christ Jesus."*

Paul, whose past was filled with violence and hate, embraced grace, set his sights on an extraordinary dream, and then gave himself totally to make that dream come true; he put muscle behind his dream because he was totally committed to it.

When Selma and I were writing this book, we were dealing with several couples who were living so far below extraordinary it seemed almost hopeless for them to experience this "beyond common" relationship.

We were discouraged and asked God, once again, to confirm the vision and passion He has placed in our lives for extraordinary marriages: "God, are we wrong?" we asked. "Is this level of marriage really possible to attain?"

Now to Him who is able to do above and beyond all that we ask or think—according to the power that works in you.
Ephesians 3:20

Embrace GRACE:
God's
Riches
At
Christ's
Expense

In the quiet and stillness of that prayerful moment, His Spirit answered, "Truth is truth, whether many or few choose it." The truth is Jesus gave His life so that you and your spouse might have life and have it more abundantly! (John 10:10) The truth is God is able to do abundantly more than you and your spouse can ask, imagine, or dream, as His power works within your marriage! (Eph. 3:20) The truth is, you can have an extraordinary marriage if you, like Paul, embrace grace, set your sights on a remarkable dream, and then commit yourselves totally to making your dream come true.

Life's big BAM! question is this: What are you going to do with the truth of Jesus Christ and the life He died to give you and your spouse?

Your response matters—to God, to you, and to others. When your marriage becomes extraordinary, it's a testimony of Him—for His honor and His glory. And the blessings that flow from that living testimony are absolutely remarkable.

For each of these extraordinary marriage benefits, write a *yes, usually, some* or *no* to describe how you are experiencing these blessings now.
- High level of respect and trust for each other _____
- Shared vision for an extraordinary marriage _____
- Planning and growing together _____
- Issues from the past resolved _____
- Strong communication, including all levels _____
- Commitment to reach full potential as a couple _____
- Experience life as an adventure with God _____
- Confidence to DREAM BIG together _____
- Serving together to impact God's Kingdom _____
- Having fun together _____
- Healthy sex life! _____
- Spiritual growth together _____

The Right Foundation

Before you put action steps to your dreams, Selma and I must reinforce a truth we began with in week 1: the true foundation of an extraordinary marriage. It's all about God.

Your desire, and that of your spouse, must be for Jesus Christ to be Lord of each of you and Lord of your marriage. Your prayer should mirror that of Paul's in Philippians 3:8 "I also consider everything to be a loss in view of the surpassing value of knowing Christ Jesus my Lord."

All of us have at one time or another leaned our ladder against the wrong wall. List some of the things you have struggled with in the past which you now consider to be of less worth than your relationship with Christ.

_____

_____

On the foundation Jesus Christ laid for us, God designed building plans for you to have an amazing relationship. That's why we included Jeremiah 29:11-12 as our verse for the week. We can't emphasize enough the importance of your believing these verses. Let them be life verses (those you claim for yourself) and remember to write in your journal ways God fulfills this promise.

Reread Jeremiah 29:11-12 on page 114. Fill in the blanks and respond to the accompanying questions.

1. God _____ the plans He has for you even when you don't know them. Why don't you know them?

_____

2. God's plan is to _____ you, not

_____ you. What do you think it means for God to

prosper you? _____

3. God's plans for you include a future filled with _____.
In what people or things do you now place your hope?

_____

4. God promises to _____ to you when you
come to Him in prayer. What can you trust God to do after

He hears your prayers? _____

Isn't it great to know that God has a very personal plan for
you and for your marriage? It's a great plan—so great, in fact,
that the impact of the extraordinary marriage He has planned
for you isn't limited to you personally. You see, your marriage
affects the world around you, and God wants to bless your
relationship so you can give Him glory and honor — and
draw others to Him.

**What do you think others can see in your marriage
now? Check all that apply.**

❏ joy   ❏ peace   ❏ cooperation   ❏ bitterness
❏ conflict   ❏ apathy   ❏ sin   ❏ forgiveness

Your children, your neighbors, your co-workers all hunger to
see extraordinary marriages. And when they see yours growing, you'll probably hear someone say to you, "I want what
you've got in your marriage." That type of response to your
marriage opens the door for you to share:

- what Jesus has done for your marriage
- what Jesus means to you personally
- how this person can have a relationship with Jesus

Your marriage direction will depend on the plans you are about to make in week 6. Now for a word of caution: As you prepare to develop your marriage plan and take action, remember who knows what's best. I (Rodney) was praying one morning and my thoughts shot ahead to the future, where I didn't know what was going to happen in a particular situation. I simply said, "God, just bless our plans." It was then that God gently thumped me on the head and reminded me that I had made plans and then asked Him to bless them.

My prayer quickly changed to "Bless us with your plan," giving the Lord the rightful place in planning for our future. God humbled me as I learned an important lesson. I should always ask the Lord to lead us in our planning, whether in life, marriage, or whatever. As you seek to make your dreams come true, remember to do the same. God is the compass of an extraordinary marriage. Asking for guidance from the One who loves you the most and truly knows what's best for you will ensure that your marriage goes in the right direction.

God is the compass of an extraordinary marriage.

Read these verses in your Bible. Answer the questions.

1. Job 42:2: Why can you be so secure in God's plan?

_____

2. Psalm 33:11: God's plan for you has been established

for how long? _____

3. Psalm 40:5: How should you respond to God's plan?

_____

4. Proverbs 16:3: How should your plans fit in with

God's plans?_____

5. Proverbs 16:9: How will God implement His plan

in your life?_____

Do You Really Want It?
The big BAM! question for life has been established (p. 116).
The question for your marriage is this: Do you really want an
extraordinary marriage? If so, how much do you want it?

How much do you want an extraordinary marriage?

Until now, Selma and I have guided your journey toward an
extraordinary marriage. Now it's your turn to take the lead.
As you focus on week 6, you and your mate are now in
charge. This week is where you as a couple need to be the
most interactive, for it ties together all you have shared and
dreamed to this point. You are ever so close to developing an
actual plan for your individual marriage!

As you set goals, make them **SMART** goals.
S—pecific. What exactly do you want to achieve?

M—easurable. How will I know I've reached my goal?

A—ttainable. Can I really reach this goal?

R—ealistic. Am I willing to work for this goal?

T—angible. Does achieving this goal have value for me?

This week is also where your marriage will show its individuality. No one will have a plan exactly like yours. That's because God has a unique plan for each and every marriage. You've dreamed about various areas of your marriage throughout the weeks of this study. Now, as you formulate your marriage plan, you'll see your marriage taking on a personality of its own. It will actually help you define your relationship with your mate.

Seeing your marriage take shape and definition through planning together can motivate you to pursue the plans that you set. And in this pursuit of spiritual, physical, and emotional growth together, you'll find the abundant-life relationship that we call an extraordinary marriage.

But before you begin to put pen to paper, take a sacred moment to again pray the prayer you said in week 1:

> *"God, we acknowledge You as the Creator and Designer of life and marriage. We need You. We know that You have an extraordinary plan for our marriage. We commit to doing whatever it takes to reach new levels of intimacy and service. Our lives and our marriage are in your hands."*

Putting It All Together

A large portion of your final group session will be *Couple Time*. As a couple, you will choose the highest priority ideas taken from your Dream Time and Marriage Plan worksheets for each week. You will choose the dreams you'd like to accomplish in the next 30 days, 60 days, and 90 days, then write these on pages 126-127.

In order to prepare for this *Couple Time* activity, look closely at the Dream Time lists and EM plan at the end of sessions one through five. Put a star by the goals that hold the most meaning for you right now. During this session, you and your spouse will agree on the goals you will write for each week's Marriage Plan Worksheet on pages 126-127.

You may find some of your Dream Time lists will have to be reduced to the smart goals we learned about on page 120. Your personal marriage plan will then take shape!

Just as a sample, on pages 124-125 we have given you the plans we made during our get-away weekend (like buy a red convertible. Just kidding!) Remember, these are our goals. Make your plan like the two of you—unique, one-of-a-kind.

Make your plan like the two of you— unique, one-of-a-kind.

Plan Guidance

At the end of session 6, you will have something 99 percent of most married couples don't have—a written marriage plan! And God will bless this effort in ways you cannot now imagine. He will take your plan and make it even better! Recall Ephesians 3:20 in the margin on page 116. Paul describes God as able to do much more than all we ask or imagine, according to His power that works in us.

After you complete this study and as you begin to work your marriage plan, be flexible with it. If necessary, make adjustments. Don't be legalistic or use your plan to brow beat each other. Rather, aim for it like you would a target.

Let it say to you: "This is where our marriage is headed. It may take longer than we expected (or not as long), but this is the direction we have set. Use the encouraging words of William Carey, the father of modern missions, as your spot light: "The future is as bright as the promises of God."

God promises you an extraordinary future when, together, you let God's power work in and through you to make your

life and your marriage all He designed it to be.
The places He will take you will be absolutely extraordinary
because He is our absolutely extraordinary God.

Parting Words
In 1920 an old rabbi was walking down the trail one night
when a young Russian guard stepped into his path and yelled,
"Halt! Who are you and where are you going?" Even with a
loaded gun pointed toward him, the old rabbi didn't panic. In
fact, he had a calm expression as he asked the young man,
"How much do they pay you?

"What?" the young guard replied in confusion.

"For this job as guard. How much do they pay you?"

The guard lowered the rifle, and his head, for he was
ashamed of how little he was getting paid. "Twenty-five
copeks a week," he said lowly.

The wise rabbi stated, "I'll pay you fifty copeks a week if,
each time I walk down this path and you see me, you will ask
me those same two questions."

As a couple, who are you and where are you going?

Do you remember what started our journey to a planned
future for our marriage? Selma asked, *"Rodney, why don't we
talk about where we would like our marriage to go?"*

May God guide you and the love of your life to frequently ask
each other:

"Where would we like our marriage to go?"

Extraordinary Marriage Plan Worksheet

	30 DAYS ACTION PLANS	60 DAYS ACTION PLAN	90 DAYS ACTION PLAN
I. Where Is Your Marriage Going?	Decide together to exercise.	Set aside two nights per week to walk together for 20 minutes.	Decide if we will continue this form of exercise or choose another.
2. Spiritual Intimacy	Ask how to pray for each other in the mornings. Then pray when we think about critical moments in each other's schedule	Pray together at bedtime. Share answers to prayer from that day.	Evaluate how this approach has helped our spiritual intimacy. Are we praying for and with each other on a more regular basis?
3. Physical Intimacy	Decide where we will go for our next romantic getaway.	Make the arrangements, remembering to clear our calendars and arrange for someone else to fill in for our ongoing responsibilities.	Have the getaway. Have fun! Implement what we have learned about men and women.

Extraordinary Marriage Plan Worksheet

SAMPLE

	30 DAYS ACTION PLANS	60 DAYS ACTION PLAN	90 DAYS ACTION PLAN
4. Emotional Intimacy	Do a "feelings check" at the end of each day. Remember not to comment in a critical way but just to listen and be there for each other.	Share a weekly meal together designed to catch up on our feelings about a variety of topics, such as work issues, parenting issues, and our relationship.	Have an "Update Date" to review our progress on this goal. Do we feel more emotionally intimate? If so, what have been the benefits?
5. Combating the Enemies	To combat busyness, "define" our calendar. Review our family calendar once a week. Look for activities that can be dropped or postponed.	Together, plan some weekly "us" time mini-retreat moments.	Designate a date, time, and place to evaluate our progress on this goal. For example, compare our schedules now to the ones 90 days ago. Are they less cluttered with non-priority activities?

Extraordinary Marriage Plan Worksheet

	30 DAYS ACTION PLANS	60 DAYS ACTION PLAN	90 DAYS ACTION PLAN
I. Where Is Your Marriage Going?			
2. Spiritual Intimacy			
3. Physical Intimacy			

Extraordinary Marriage Plan Worksheet

	30 DAYS ACTION PLANS	60 DAYS ACTION PLAN	90 DAYS ACTION PLAN
4. Emotional Intimacy			
5. Combating the Enemies			

Once you have completed your 90 day Extraordinary Marriage plan, don't stop. Dream bigger dreams. Repeat the process, but this time, add a 1 year action plan. The more you put your goals down on paper, you will find that planning can become a regular part of your relationship. And that's EXTRAORDINARY!

How to Use the Leader Guide

Extraordinary Marriage: God's Plan for Your Journey Leader Guide will equip you to facilitate a unique marriage enrichment experience. Each session plan provides several activities for a 1 to 1 1/2 hour session. As the group leader, you will need to choose activities according to time parameters and group characteristics.

We recommend you purchase the accompanying *DVD & CD-ROM Pack* (ISBN 0-6331-9802-1) for this study. The DVD contains seven 8-10 minute presentations by authors Rodney and Selma Wilson, who give a preview and offer motivation for each topic.

The CD-ROM includes worksheets, devotionals for both men and women, and leader tips—ways to make group time energizing and engaging. Neither the CD-ROM nor the DVD is essential to completing the course.

The member book contains an introduction and six weeks of individual study. With an introductory session, you will be providing a seven-session group experience. Many of the leader guide activities and questions have suggested answers in parentheses. Use these as prompters, summaries, or additions to group responses. Group activities and worksheets have already been formatted for your use on pages 148-158.

Preparation is a must for successful group interaction. The time you spend praying over and planning for each session will be obvious to the members of your study group. Leader Guide suggestions for each group session are divided into two categories.

Before the Session

A checklist includes all the information you need to prepare in advance for the group session. Prompts are given when optional video and group activities can be found on the DVD and CD-ROM.

During the Session

Suggestions include *Warm Up* activities to get the members focused on the content for each session; *In the Word* Bible study for Scriptures relating to the session topic; *Book Talk* to review the member book content, and *Couple Talk* to encourage couples to process what they've learned in an emotionally safe environment.

This study will lead members to develop a plan for their own extraordinary marriages—real plans and real strategies.

Members will build their plans week to week and will refine them during the last session. Model the role by working on your own marriage plan.

Ask your spouse to participate or serve as a co-leader so that both male and female voices are heard. Ask a couple to participate whom you can train as leaders of the next *Extraordinary Marriage* study.

Begin your publicity and prayer chain six weeks before the study begins. Because of the topic, publicize the study to couples who might not come for a regular Bible study. Adults who are unchurched can be reached for salvation and for church membership. Be up front about the biblical content. God's Word is the key to an extraordinary marriage.

Introductory Session

Before the Session

1. Pray—
2. Prepare—
"Celebrating a Century of Marriage" Decorate a flip chart page or poster with a wedding theme and the title, "Celebrating a Century of Marriage." You will need space to record how many years members have been married. Participants will share this information during the session. Then, you will total the column(s).

"Wall of Wisdom"—Create a poster that represents a wall with the title printed at the top. Display it as a way for members to share words of wisdom about marriage. Have 3x5 cards and masking tape or self-adhesive notes for each participant.

"Window on Expectations" (p.148)— Supply three small self-adhesive dots for each person. You will find instructions in step 5 of *Warm Up*.

(optional) Overview cards—If you are not using the DVD, write key points from this study on 3x5 cards. Key points can be found in week titles, margin statements, or sub-heads from each week's material.

3. Arrange—
Audiovisual equipment for DVD
Seating in a semi-circle facing a display wall with moveable chairs.

4. Supply—
Attendance sheet (p. 159)—Duplicate for this study or download the one on the CD-ROM.
Name tags (optional)
Marker board and markers, eraser
Flip chart, tear sheets or posters, markers, and masking tape
Member books (one for each person) and payment process

During the Session

1. As participants arrive, ask each to sign the attendance sheet, take a name tag, and pick up and pay for a member book for *Extraordinary Marriage: God's Plan for Your Journey.*

2. Welcome members and begin the session on time. Start with prayer.

Warm-Up

1. Display the "Celebrating a Century of Marriage" poster. As participants introduce themselves, ask them to tell how many years they have been married. If a couple has been married ten years, each of them adds 10 years to the total. They are credited with 20 years as a couple.

2. After all have shared their years of marriage, add the numbers and write the sum on the poster.

3. Introduce yourself. Write the number of years you've been married beside the sum total on the poster. (Your spouse's number should already be in the sum total.) Use the difference between the numbers to show that you are not the marriage expert. You will guide them through the study in a way that draws on their many years of collective wisdom.

4. Distribute a 3 x 5 card or large sticky note to each person. To prove the value of their collective wisdom and experience, ask each member to think of a "word of wisdom" about marriage—something they might share with someone about to be married.

Instruct them to write their thoughts on the card or note and place it on the poster "Wall of Wisdom." (Example: "When she says, 'Nothing's wrong,' don't believe it." or "Don't leave home without kissing your spouse.")

Encourage everyone to have fun, but caution them not to embarrass their spouses. (It's wise to have each spouse approve the other's wisdom card before it's displayed!) After participants have posted the cards or notes, encourage volunteers to read their words of wisdom aloud to the group.

5. Ask the group to turn to "Window on Expectations" (p. 148). Distribute three self-adhesive dots to each person. Have members place their dots in the window panes that represent their top three expectations for this study. Then, call out the name of each window pane and record the number of dots it received. Announce the top three vote-getters. Keep these in mind as you plan future sessions.

One option for this activity is to give members red dots at the beginning of the study. At the conclusion of the study, give members blue dots to represent what they actually experienced during the study.

6. Introduce the authors, Rodney and Selma Wilson (p. 4). If you purchased the Leader Kit, play the introductory session of the DVD. Ask members to open the Member Book to the Table of Contents (p. 3) and follow along as the Wilsons preview the study.

7. If you are not using the DVD, overview the study beginning with pages 3-4 of the member book. Highlight key points from the introduction on pages 6-9. Suggest that persons look through the book searching for key points.

An energizing way to introduce key points is to write overview statements on numbered 3 x 5 cards (one statement per card). Distribute them to volunteers and suggest they be read in numbered order.

In the Word

1. Point out that the Bible has much advice for husbands and wives. Remind the group that a chapter or verse does not have to mention the word *marriage* to be applicable.

2. Ask members to locate Philippians 3:12-15 in their Bibles. Read each verse aloud and ask the suggested questions.

Verse 12—What applications do we see for life and for marriage?
(Possible responses:
- Life/marriage processes toward goals.
- Life/marriage is a journey, and we haven't reached the end of it yet.
- The journey requires effort on our part. An extraordinary life or marriage won't happen automatically.
- When we know Christ, He makes an eternal difference in our journey.)

Verse 13—In life and marriage, why is it beneficial to pursue goals?
(Possible responses:
- Keeps our direction focused
- Establishes priorities
- Helps minimize chaos
- Increases peace and harmony
- Keeps both spouses on same page.)

Emphasize that this study is unique in that members will look toward the future, instead of focusing on where their marriages have been. Members will learn the benefits of creating a vision for their own extraordinary marriages tailored to their personal dreams and goals.

Verse 14—What are the blessings of living life God's way? (When we live life God's way, especially in our marriages, life is better than anything we could dream. We have the added blessings of designing our marriages by God's plan.)

Verse 15—Invite members to pray for the next six weeks that God will grow and mature their relationship to Him and to one another. Ask them to pray that God will reveal His perfect plans for their marriages during this study.

Book Talk

1. Explain the format of the member book. Couples should buy two books so that each person can respond to the learning activities. Point out an example in week 1 (p. 15). Books include prompts for couples to share thoughts with one another during the week or during group sessions.

2. Activities are designed to provide Bible study, personal reflection, and time for prayer. Encourage members to pace themselves by studying part of the week's lesson each day.

3. Explain the four segments of group sessions: *Warm Up, In the Word, Book Talk, Couple Talk.*

4. Encourage members to read the Introduction on pages 6-9 as soon as they get home! Then read week 1.

5. Before the next session, each person should complete the Personal Strengths

Assessment (pp. 27-29). Invite couples to discuss their results with each other during the week.

Couple Talk

1. Ask couples to sit knee to knee looking at each other. Tell them each session will end this way in order for them to process the information with each other. This position will become more comfortable as the study proceeds.

2. For today, ask them to affirm their commitment to each other and to this study. Allow time for couples to talk.

3. Close the session in prayer.

Session 1

Before the Session

1. Pray—
2. Prepare—
"The Religious Practices of Adult Believers"(CD-ROM)—If you didn't purchase the Kit, prepare a flip chart page or poster with statistics from the Barna survey on pages 11-12.

Provide paper, pens or pencils, and extra Bibles as needed.

3. Arrange—
Audiovisual equipment
Seating in movable chairs
4. Supply—
Attendance Sheet and Name Tags
Extra Member Books, Bibles

During the Session

1. As they arrive, ask members to sign the attendance sheet and wear a name tag (optional).

2. Introduce newcomers to the group and ask them to tell about themselves. In turn, have members introduce themselves.

3. Begin class on time with prayer.

Warm-Up

1. Play session 1 of the DVD(optional).

2. Introduce the "Marriage Metaphors" activity on page 149. Explain that a metaphor compares one idea or object to another, such as "time is money." Provide an example of a marriage metaphor, such as marriage is a pop quiz because you never know when your spouse will ask a BAM question. Ask members to complete the four statements on their own.

Prompters might include traveling terms such as marriage is a journey, bridge, highway, scenic route, rest stop, map, billboard, or road sign.

Provide the following rules:
• Don't embarrass your spouse.
• Be positive and creative.

3. After members finish the activity, ask spouses to share their metaphors with each other before sharing with the group.

4. Emphasize that all of our marriages are going somewhere. Ask, Why would we want to shape that direction?

In the Word

1. Explain that Proverbs is known as the Book of Wisdom. Review Solomon's request for wisdom from God. (See 2 Chron. 1:7-13).

2. Point out Proverbs 4:26 on page 10 Ask, Why does this bit of wisdom from Solomon apply to marriage?

3. Brainstorm ways we can know we are on level ground with a firm foundation. List responses on a marker board or poster. Then ask, How would this knowledge benefit a marriage?

Book Talk

1. Ask, What direction do you think marriage in American culture is headed?

2. Review some of the statistics given in week 1 (pp. 11-12) or use the CD-ROM visual. Invite comments as to what factors contribute to these statistics.

3. Explain that while these statistics are startling, they are reversible. Brainstorm how we can reduce negative marriage statistics and increase positive ones (1) as individuals? (2) as couples? (3) as a church? (4) as a society? Write responses on a marker board or tear sheet.

4. Discuss the activity on page 13. Ask, Why is planning helpful in the areas you listed? What happens if we don't plan?

5. Remind members that the primary outcome of this study is to help each couple build a step-by-step marriage plan together, with Rodney and Selma's help.

Explain that by the end of the study, couples will have completed a plan to accomplish immediate, short-term, and long-range goals in several categories. This plan is on pages 126-127. You will fill in your plan during session seven.

6. Form small groups of 2-3 couples. Invite members to open to the activity sheet, "When We Get Together," on page 150. This activity is based on the Personal Strengths Assessment. Assign groups one or two combinations of personal strengths such as Lion and Beaver.

Ask someone from each group to read the directions. After allowing adequate time, regain the attention of the groups and have them report their conclusions.

Couple Talk

1. Ask couples to arrange their chairs so that they can sit knee to knee. Explain the assignment on page 25 by giving these instructions.

(1) Review your responses to the Preferred Future chart (p. 18)

(2) Review your responses to the Dream Time check list (p. 22).

(3) On page 25, from your lists, write ideas/activities you agree on and believe you can accomplish within each of these time periods.

- 30 days (immediate goals)
- 60 days (short-term goals)
- 90 days (long-range goals)

Couples will add to their plan sheets each week and then discuss them during

Couple Time, making needed adjustments.

2. Call attention to page 26. Explain that knowing for sure that you are a Christian will prepare you for week 2, "Do You Know Each Other by Heart ... and Soul?"

4. Close the session in prayer.

Session 2

Before the Session

1. Pray—
2. Prepare—

Moldable Marriage—You will need a walnut-size piece of modeling or craft clay for each member. Put each piece in a small plastic bag to distribute during the session. Have wet-wipes available to clean hands and a small trash bag for disposal.

3. Arrange and supply necessary materials and equipment for activities.

During the Session

Warm Up

1. Welcome members, direct them to the attendance sheet, and begin the session on time with prayer.

2. Have members turn to the inside of the back cover of their member books (or on sheets of paper). Ask couples to create an Affirmation Acrostic by writing their spouses' first names vertically and listing endearing characteristics that begin with the appropriate letter.

Give this example using the author's names. Read or write it on a tear sheet.

S—ensitive	R—espectful
E—nergetic	O—pen
L—oving	D—evoted
M—erry	N—urturing
A—ffirming	E—ncouraging
	Y—oung-at-heart

3. After members have completed the activity, ask them to share their acrostics with their mates.

4. Distribute pieces of modeling clay. Ask participants to remove the clay from the bag and begin "working it." As they handle the clay, molding and shaping it, ask, What does it take to shape a piece of clay into something beautiful or useful? Write their responses on a flip chart or wallboard. (Possible responses:

- It must be soft, not hardened, pliable,
- Stay in the molded shape.
- It needs someone to shape it.
- The molder has to have some skill in shaping it.
- The molder has to have a vision for what shape the clay will take.)

5. Explain that this session will help us understand how God wants to shape us and our marriages. Collect the clay samples and distribute wet-wipes if needed.

6. Play the session 2 video (optional).

In the Word

1. Ask everyone to locate page 151, the "Week 2: Scripture Search." Encourage everyone to take notes as the group

examines these three Scripture passages. They are to recognize that God is the potter (molder of the clay), and then picture their marriages as the clay (the medium to be shaped).

2. Select someone to read aloud Isaiah 29:16. Ask, Do people get the Potter and the clay (Creator-created) relationship regarding marriage turned around? Why?(Our culture today minimizes the sanctity of marriage and we choose to define marriage by man's standards rather than God's.)

3. Ask, In what ways do people deny God's creative power in marriages? In what ways do they deny God's ownership of marriage? (Civil unions, high divorce rates, "alternative" forms of marriage, and leaving God out of the home.)

4. Some people don't believe that God cares about them, understands them or their marriage situations. Ask, In what ways do people demonstrate this faulty perception about God? When people believe that God is impersonal or distant, they don't pray to Him about their marriages, they don't seek the counsel of His Word, and they don't put Christ at the center of their marriage. They turn to the ways of the world to seek understanding.

5. Read Isaiah 45:9. Ask, How might we be guilty of arguing with our Maker at times? Help participants understand that sometimes we question how God has fashioned marriage. We doubt His hand in our circumstances.

Ask, When we argue with God, what are we saying to Him? (To argue with God is a form of mistrust, and to mistrust God is disobedience. When we argue with God we are saying, "I don't trust You, but I trust my own way." This is sin.)

6. Read Jeremiah 18:1-4. Focus on the last verse. Ask, What principle from this verse can we apply to marriage? (When our marriages become flawed, God doesn't want them cast away or destroyed. Just as the potter re-works flawed clay, God will re-work, reshape and refine our marriages if we trust the Potter's hand.)

7. Remind members of the clay activity. Ask, What will it take for God to be able to shape a marriage? (Some of the same responses apply. Our hearts must remain soft and moldable under the Potter's hand. We must trust the vision and plan that He has for our for our lives. Clay doesn't mold itself. We cannot shape an extraordinary marriage without His help.)

Book Talk

1. Review the meaning of the Intimate Equation on page 33.

2. Ask, What are some of our responsibilities in developing intimacy with God? (Paying attention to God's presence, listening to Him, drawing near to Him and seeking Him. We have to desire a close relationship to God.)

3. Ask, What are the marriage benefits of nurturing an intimate relationship with God? (We can give abundantly to our

spouses. When we are spiritually depleted, we have little to give to our spouses.)

4. Review the spiritual disciplines listed on pages 40-43. Discuss with members how well they think most Christians develop these disciplines. Then discuss which of the spiritual disciplines might contribute the most to the making of strong marriages.

Couple Talk

1. Instruct couples to arrange seating to sit knee-to-knee to share their individual responses to the last activity on page 44. Ask couples to share what they want to do to improve in areas of spiritual discipline and what they want to pray for in their marriages.

2. Direct couples' attention to the Dream Time list on page 48. Instruct couples to examine their joint lists and determine which activities to place on their 30 day, 60 day and 90 day planning sheet on page 49. Explain that couples will add those ideas/activities to their Extraordinary Marriage Plan Worksheet in session 7.

3. Close the session in prayer.

Session 3

Before the Session

1. Pray—
2. Prepare—
"Recipe for Romance" (CD-ROM)—

If you do not have the Kit, bring a recipe card for each member. On a flip chart, poster, or overhead transparency, list the parts of a recipe:
- ingredients
- mixing directions
- additional preparations
- yield (how many or how much)

Review the "Love T-Chart" (page 152), "Building Openness" (page 153) and "Design the Date of the Century" (page 154).

3. Have available tear sheets or poster board with markers.

4. Arrange and set up necessary materials and equipment for activities.

During the Session

Warm Up

1. Welcome members, direct them to sign the attendance sheet, and begin the session on time with prayer.

2. Show the session 3 video. (optional)

3. Remind members of the saying, "Sex starts in the kitchen." Explain that they will engage in an activity, "Recipe for Romance," with that in mind! Divide members into smaller groups of 4-6, making sure every group has both men and women but not spouses (if possible).

4. Distribute the recipe cards. Display the Parts of a Recipe poster or use the worksheet from the CD-ROM. Suggest members find each of these parts on the recipe card they are holding.

5. Read Romans 12:9-18. From this passage, ask groups to design a recipe for a romantic marriage relationship, using each of the recipe parts. Give groups a tear sheet or poster and marker to write the group's recipe.

Add more fun by having a competition for the best recipe and providing a small prize to the winning group's members. Call for group reports when time is up.

In the Word

1. Ask members to turn to the chart on page 152. Explain that true love possesses certain qualities whether the love is romantic, between other family members, between believers, or the kind of love we are to have for the lost. The focus of this activity will be to use the biblical principles of love and apply it to the marriage relationship.

2. Ask members to locate in their Bibles 1 Corinthians 13:4-7. As you read the passage aloud, ask members to listen for the qualities love requires and for what love will relinquish. Then invite volunteers to suggest words for each side of the chart. (Example: patience under Requires; envy under Relinquishes) As each of you complete the chart, tell couples they will use their charts later in the session.

3. When the chart is completed ask individuals silently to review the list and put a check before the qualities of love that would have a direct affect on physical

intimacy. Allow 1-2 minutes for each person to check his/her list privately.

Book Talk

1. Play the session video. (optional) Invite members to turn to page 63 and find the quote by Alan Loy McGinnis. Select someone to read the quote aloud. Say, When couples find themselves far apart, openness is a key factor in drawing them closer together again. Sometimes it's difficult to initiate openness after a period of being apart.

2. Invite the group to turn to *Building Openness* on page 153. Remind members that they indicated their degree of openness in the activity on page 51. This activity will provide ways to increase openness and will highlight key principles contained in this study.

3. Ask the group to suggest words for each letter. As each letter is completed, ask an appropriate question. Possible responses and questions are given to help you guide discussion.

O—(ffer unconditional love). How would you define unconditional love?

P—(ray for one another and pray together.) How does prayer increase openness between a couple?

E—(xpress emotions honestly.) What cautions should we consider when expressing emotions to our spouses?

N—(urture trust.) What are the ways we nurture trust in marriage?

N—(avigate around barriers.) Can you

name three primary barriers to intimacy among most couples?

E—(liminate unloving thoughts and actions.) What are some ways we can close down openness in marriage?

S—(avor intimate moments.) Can you list one or more ideas for increasing private time for couples?

S—(afeguard the sanctity of the marriage relationship.) What are some ways each spouse can safeguard his/her marriage?

4. (optional)Divide members into groups of 4-5 men only and 4-5 women only. Ask groups to create their own top ten romantic ideas by brainstorming ways to enliven the marriage relationship. Suggestions will not be presented to the entire group, but each person should take notes somewhere in week 3 or on their own paper.

This activity will help couples initiate new ideas by learning from each other. As groups develop their lists of the top ten romantic ideas, encourage members to exercise confidentiality.

Couple Talk

1. If you used optional activity 4 from Book Talk, ask members to move to the knee-to-knee position. Each spouse will have his or her list of romantic ideas in writing but without names. Direct couples to use their lists to generate ideas they agree to try—or to be more intentional about—in their physical relationship.

2. Using these ideas and adding to them from their Dream Time lists on pages 66-67, encourage each couple to design the perfect romantic date—for them. *Design the Date of the Century* on page 154 asks some key questions.

After couple's reflect and answer the questions, if you want to have them share ideas, ask only volunteers. Date ideas may be too private for sharing with the large group.

3. Instruct couples to work together to fill in their mutual goals on page 69.

4. In concluding the session, ask individuals to close their eyes for a time of reflection. Suggest that each individual assess how well he or she is doing in the areas covered by their "Recipe for Romance." How many of the qualities that love requires do they demonstrate, and which relinquished thoughts and actions have they truly given up?

5. Close with prayer.

Session 4

Before the Session

1. Pray—

2. Prepare—

"Relighting the Unity Candle" (CD-ROM)—Prior to the session, ask a couple in this study to help you re-enact the Unity Candle ceremony performed in many weddings. If you didn't purchase the Kit, perhaps your pastor can provide you a copy of a Unity Candle Ceremony. If you design your own, incorporate Romans 15:5 and Colossians 3:14. Obtain 3 candles (one tall candle and two shorter candles). Light the two shorter candles so they are burning when members begin arriving. Play wedding music in the background before and after the DVD.

Review the following worksheets:
"Masking Emotions" (page 155)
"Guardrails" (page 156)
"I Know You Like a Book"—CD-ROM

3. Arrange and set up necessary materials and equipment.

During the Session

Warm Up

1. Welcome members, direct them to sign attendance sheets, and begin the session on time with prayer. Turn off the wedding music briefly.

2. Play the session 4 video. (optional)

3. Prepare for the Unity Candle ceremony. Dim the lights if possible. Turn on the music, playing it softly in the background.

4. Instruct members to listen for statements in the ceremony which describe how the couple is to be unified. What areas of their lives will be affected?

5. Ask the enlisted couple to stand behind the candles so as not to block the vision of the others. As you read through the service, prompt the couple to light the unity candle with the two shorter candles that represent their individual lives.

When the unity candle is burning, each will extinguish his or her own candle.

6. At the conclusion of the ceremony, ask members to share from their observations. Summarize that the marriage relationship is designed to unite couples physically, emotionally, and spiritually.

7. Ask the group to find Ephesians 4:3 in their Bibles. Read the passage aloud. Ask, Who is the source of this unity? Point out that real unity in a marriage, or in any relationship, comes from the Spirit and the peace of Christ that binds any Christ-centered relationship together.

8. Brainstorm the character traits of a person unified with the Spirit. Make the point that these characteristics should be true of Christian marriage partners, as well as believers in general.

9. Invite someone to review Selma's story at the beginning of week 4. (During much of her mother's illness, she and Rodney were away from one another. Yet their marriage relationship maintained unity.) Ask, How did they maintain unity? How does emotional intimacy lead to unity in a marriage?

10. Discuss the connection between a person's level of communication with God and his/her comfort level with emotional intimacy—with unity—in marriage.

In the Word

1. Explain that Jesus expressed a full range of emotions perfectly because He was in perfect connection with the Father.

Lead members to locate John 11:17, 32-37 in their Bibles. (Different translations vary considerably in the description of Jesus' emotions in this passage. Because it is a highly accurate translation, Holman CSB version is recommended.)

2. Read the passage aloud. Discuss the circumstances of this passage. (Lazarus has been dead for four days and his sisters, Mary and Martha, are grieving.) Then lead the group to identify two emotions attributed to Jesus (v.s 32-33).

3. Ask, Did Jesus express both of these emotions openly? (No, only compassion or grief.) Make the point that Jesus displayed His compassion openly because he felt genuine grief. His reaction ministered to Mary and Martha. Ask, What effect did the expression of His grief have on others? (Some recognized His genuine love and grief. Others criticized His absence during Lazarus' illness.)

4. Read verses 38-44. Note that Jesus didn't openly display His anger. Instead, He took action. He was not motivated to act out of His emotional feelings. He acted to display God's glory and increase the faith of those observing. Jesus did not sin in His anger.

5. (Optional, depending on time) Invite a volunteer to read Luke 19:41 as another example of Jesus' grief. Then, read Luke:19:45-48 and explain why Jesus' anger is justified. (Jesus has heavenly authority to rebuke the people for their disregard and desecration of God's

temple.) Ask, Why should we exercise extreme caution in the display of our anger? (Our anger is not usually righteous indignation.) Point out that Jesus felt emotion deeply, yet His emotions did not control Him. He always acted from higher motives than the emotions He felt.

6. Say, Jesus did something spectacular with His emotions. He laid them bare; then He laid them down before the Father. Jesus relinquished His feelings and carried out His Father's will (Matthew 26:36-46). Yet, He didn't wear masks before God or His disciples pretending He was unaffected by the situations He encountered.

Book Talk

1. Select a volunteer to read the quote by Calvin Miller on page 74.

2. From page 75 of week 4, invite members to name the emotional masks they identified in the first activity. Instruct everyone to write these on the left column of the worksheet, "Masking Emotions" on page 155.

Then move to the right side of the chart. As time permits, brainstorm effects of these masks on emotional intimacy in marriage.

3. (Optional) "I Know You Like a Book"—CD-ROM. Direct members' attention to the first two paragraphs on page 76 of week 4. Distribute the worksheet and follow the directions.

If you do not have the worksheet, play a type of newly-wed game that requires a spouse to guess answers such as the spouses' favorite color, flower, and so on.

4. Discuss the two guardrails in week 4. Ask, Can you think of other guardrails that protect the emotional unity and intimacy in marriage? How do they help?

5. Summarize the guardrails mentioned by the group. Invite the group to turn to page 156, "Guardrails," and take notes as the group discusses the guardrails that have not been listed.) Possible responses:

• **Read Signals.** Observe your mate well enough to read his/her emotional signals. Sensing your mate's frustration, worry, fear, and anxiety is the first step toward being connected.

• **Respond Lovingly.** When your mate shares with you at a deep emotional level, your response can contribute to his or her emotional security. A loving response builds intimacy.

• **Refresh One Another.** Often! Find ways to give comfort, encouragement, and emotional support. STAND IN THE GAP when your spouse especially needs prayer.

• **Resist Temptation.** Hebrews 13:4 says, "Honor marriage, and guard the sacredness of sexual intimacy between wife and husband. God draws a firm line against casual and illicit sex (The Message).

• **Rekindle the Home Fires.** Read Proverbs 5:18-20. God's very own word instructs those who are married to keep the marriage bed warm!

Couple Talk

1. Before couples sit knee to knee, instruct them to reflect individually on their responses to the Emotional Intimacy Assessment they completed in week 4 (pp.. 82-83). After the time for reflection, ask couples to sit knee-to-knee to share what they learned about themselves.

2. Then ask couples to discuss ways to increase the percentage of straight talk in their relationship (p. 86). Direct them to combine this discussion with their responses to the Dream Time list on page 88

3. As they determine priorities, tell them to add these plans to the worksheet on page 89. Which ideas can be accomplished in (1) 30 days; (2) 60 days (3) 90 days?

4. Close the session with prayer.

Session 5

Before the Session

1. Pray—
2. Prepare—
In this session, as you form groups, change members of the groups from one activity to another to build relationships and add variety.

"Dimes and Dragons"—Provide a large poster or tear sheet and colored markers for each group of 4-6 members. Be prepared to give a dime to each group.

"The Case of the Disguised Dragon" (CD-ROM)—Prepare an envelope for each group of 4-6 members. Put one case study from the CD-ROM in each envelope. If you do not have the Kit, write four or five case studies yourself—scenarios of couples who are struggling with "lurking dragons." Focus on a different dragon in each case study. On each envelope write its case study number (Case # ____).

The CD-ROM contains a leader debriefing guide to help you lead the discussion that follows the case studies. Provide a small treat for the winning team (optional).

Review these worksheets.

"Dragon Slayers Unite!"—page 157. Follow the directions given on the page.

"Scripture Search"—page 158

3. Arrange and set up necessary materials and equipment for activities.

During the Session

Warm Up

1. Welcome members and direct them to sign the attendance sheet. Begin the session on time with prayer.

2. Divide members into groups of 4 (2 couples). Provide the paper and markers for the "Dimes and Dragons" activity. Instruct groups to lay their papers on a flat surface where they can draw 2 large circles—one above the other in the center of the sheet.

Explain their assignment. As a team, they are to draw in as many details of the head (top circle) and tail (bottom circle) sides of a dime from memory. They can't

look at a dime from their pockets or purses. They are to draw the dimes from memory.

When group members remember a detail, one member should draw it on the correct side of the coin. Give only 5 minutes for this activity. At the end of the time period, ask groups to display their pictures.

Groups can then look at a dime to evaluate the pictures. Consider giving small prizes to the members of the group with the most accurately drawn details.

3. Ask a series of questions to debrief the activity. How many times in a week do most people handle a dime? How many details were missed by most groups? How can the details of something handled as frequently as a dime be overlooked so easily? (Sometimes when something grows so familiar, we begin to take it for granted, miss the details.) Ask, How does this activity relate to the dragons that find comfortable niches in our homes? Do we tend to recognize dragons in somebody else's home more easily than in our own? Why?

4. Prepare for *The Case of the Disguised Dragon* activity. Change group membership. Explain that dragons disguise themselves so they can roam about our homes undetected, wreaking havoc between unsuspecting spouses. In this activity, each group of 4-6 members will receive a dossier (envelop) profiling a couple being held as unknowing hostages by one or more dastardly dragons.

Their assignment will be to (1) gain entrance into the couple's home, (2) identify the camouflaged beast(s), (3) design an extraction strategy, and (4) before leaving the home, leave their calling card—a Scripture passage for the couple to protect their home.

5. Distribute the envelopes. Allow time for groups to discuss and plan their strategy. After groups finish and come back to headquarters (large group), lead a debriefing discussion. For groups that find appropriate Scriptures, give each member a small treat.

In the Word

1. Play the session 5 video. (optional)

2. Read together Ephesians 6:10-18. Divide members into different groups of 4-6 members for *Dragon Slayers Unite!* on page 157. Instruct groups to match dragons to the piece of armor that would most effectively eradicate them. (For example, poor self esteem might be listed next to Belt of Truth, because the truth of who we are comes only from the Word of God.)

Allow time for groups to place at least two dragons next to each piece of armor. To debrief the activity, ask the group spokespersons to read one or more examples from their group's work and discuss their answers.

2. Explain that the best Dragon Slayer is the Prince of Peace! When Christ rules in our homes, peace will reign in our hearts. When we find the courage to face our dragons and hand them their eviction notices, we need to fill up the spaces they occupied.

3. Display the verses listed below or give a copy to members. Lead members to analyze the verses to determine what can fill the voids left by evicted dragons. Select someone to read each verse in order. Then ask the questions after each verse is read. If time is limited, choose only some of the verses to discuss.

Proverbs 12:20. How does promoting peace in our home bring joy?

John 16:33. How will we find Christ's peace in the midst of normal trials and sufferings?

Philippians 4:9. How does our disobedience/obedience to God affect the degree of peace we experience.

John 14:27. How exactly does Christ's peace differ from the world's peace?

Romans 14:19. What are ways we promote peace in our homes?

Hebrews 12:11. How does God's discipline for our disobedience ultimately result in peace?

Book Talk

1. Review the kind of damage the Busyness Dragon does to marriages (pp. 97-101). Brainstorm ideas to help us prioritize our competing responsibilities.

2. Review the "ousting strategies" listed on page 104. Consider bringing samples of books or Bible studies that relate to several dragons to spark interest in a later

study. Use the address on page 2 to order a current catalog of products from LifeWay Church Resources.

3. Review the discussion of unresolved conflict on pages 104-108. On page 108 highlight the key principles of processing conflict.

Couple Talk

1. As couples sit knee-to-knee, direct them to compare their responses to the following activities in the book:
- Establish Our Night activity (p. 99).
- Overhaul Our Family's Schedule (p. 100).
- Dream Time activity. Ask them to add specifics to the ones they agree on, assigning dates, time lines, or how-to strategies.

2. Ask them to record decisions on the plan worksheet on page 113.

3. Encourage couples to put action to this study by completing week 6. This week will bring everything together and provide couples the opportunity to refine their hopes and dreams.

4. Close the session with prayer.

Session 6

Before the Session
1. Pray—
2. Prepare—
(optional) "What's In An Extraordinary Marriage?" (CD-ROM)—If you do not have the Kit, prepare a sheet of paper for each couple with the words "What's in an Extraordinary Marriage?" at the top. Divide the number of sheets into 3 sets of one page each. On one set of sheets, write these directions: *You have 5 minutes to find 25 words in Extraordinary Marriage. Words can be formed by taking letters from each of the title words.*

On the second set of the sheets change the number from 25 to 35. On the last set of sheets change the number to 50. The object of the activity is to see how many couples will simply stop working when they've achieved the expectation—the stated number of words.

(optional) "Puzzle-Piece Processing" (CD-ROM)—If you don't have the master available on CD-ROM, draw a large rectangle on a poster. Divide the rectangle into 7 irregular, curved pieces—puzzle pieces that fit together. On each puzzle piece write the title of one of the six weeks studied. Leave one puzzle piece toward the center blank. Cut the puzzle pieces apart. Prepare tape pieces or adhesive so puzzle pieces can be affixed to the poster and reassembled to complete the original puzzle.

3. Arrange and set up equipment.

During the Session

Warm Up

1. Welcome members and thank them for being faithful to the last session. Begin

the session on time with prayer.

2. Distribute the "What's in An Extraordinary Marriage" sheets. Give one sheet to each couple to work on together. Be sure to mix up the sheets so some with each of the three sets of directions circulate to the couples. Explain that you will not go over the directions verbally. The directions are written on each couple's sheet, and they should follow those directions in silence.

The challenge is to keep the group from knowing there are 3 different sets of directions. You want them to assume they are all working on the same assignment.

State general rules: Words can be formed from both title words. You can only use as many letters in your words as appears in the title. (Example r is repeated but there is only one d). Keep your eyes on your own paper!!!

Give exactly 5 minutes for couples to list their words. Call "time" and make sure everyone stops writing words. Ask how many words each couple found. After reports are given, determine if anyone exceeded their written expectations.

Then compare the numbers couples wrote compared to their instructions. It is likely that when those with Instruction #1 found 25 words, they stopped. When those with Instruction #2 found 35 they stopped and so on.

Ask, How many times do we only do what's expected and no more? When we accomplish what is expected of us we are

generally satisfied with our results. Ask, What do you think this has to do with pursuing an extraordinary marriage? Lead members to see that if they expect ordinary, that's what they'll have. But if they expect—and strive for—an extraordinary marriage, it is well within their grasp.

In the Word / Book Talk (combined)

1. Review the Scripture search activities on pages 117-120 and solicit member responses. Focus on how our plans are successful only when they begin with God's plans and fit into His plan at every stage. Remind couples to prayerfully seek God's guidance as they refine and implement their plans.

2. Transition the group to a time of reflection on all they've learned and experienced. Play the session 6 video.

3. (optional) Direct them to the "Puzzle Piece Processing" activity (CD-ROM). Hold up the first puzzle piece with the title of the first week. Ask, What were the key principles you learned in week 1? Allow members to glance back through their books and glean some of the major points studied. Affix the puzzle piece to the puzzle board (wall or poster). As each week is highlighted, they will see the puzzle coming together.

Point out that one puzzle piece is blank. Ask the group to speculate on the title of that piece. Answers will vary, but lead the group to understand that each of them is critical to the completion of the puzzle.

God has designed this beautiful master-piece that sometimes looks like a puzzle to us. But God puts it all together. We have to decide to fit into His plan to complete the picture of an extraordinary | marriage. It doesn't happen without our individual commitment.

Couple Talk

1. Allow extra time for couples to work together to fill in their plans for this study based on the Dream Time and plan worksheets from previous weeks. They will need to select the goals with the highest priorities to place on the Marriage Plan Worksheet on pages 126-127.

2. If needed, be available to help them as they work. This process may take more time than allotted. If so, encourage couples to complete this final challenge at home in the near future. Do not place any pressure on finishing at this time.

3. (optional) Plan an eighth session at a future date so that couples can share their plans with each other. This session would encourage couples to finish their work and draw inspiration from other couples.

Group Closure

To wrap up the study, instruct members to locate Matthew 7:7-11 in their Bibles. Call on a volunteer to read these verses aloud. Make these statements or copy this paragraph for all to read.

These verses give us permission to ask for an extraordinary marriage, to work for it, to search for all that God has designed for us in marriage. We must persevere by continuing to knock, and God will open the door to blessings beyond anything we can even imagine. God's plan for an extraordinary marriage never ends and neither should ours. With each passing year, we should commit to renew, refine and refresh our plans with the amazing power of God's creative Holy Spirit.

Stand in a circle and join hands. Allow volunteers to share what they liked best or learned from this study. Sing a familiar praise song and invite sentence prayers. Close the prayer by asking God's blessings on each couple as they work toward the goal of an extraordinary marriage.

WORKSHEETS

These worksheets are to be used during group sessions and are not for individual use.

Introduction: Window on Expectations

Session 1:   Marriage Metaphors

When We All Get Together

Session 2:   Scripture Search

Session 3:   Love Requires/Relinquishes

Building Openness

Design the Date of the Century

Session 4:   Masking Emotions

Guardrails

Session 5:   Dragon Slayers Unite

Scripture Search

Introduction: Window on Expectations

Using your colored dots, pick your top three expectations.

New Information	**Inspiration**	**Couple Time**
Learning from others	**Fellowship with couples**	**Strengthen our Marriage**
Removing barriers	**Practical skills**	**Other**

Session 1: Marriage Metaphors

Marriage is

_____

because

_____

Marriage is

_____

because

_____

Marriage is

_____

because

_____

Marriage is

_____

because

_____

Session 1: When We Get Together

Your study leader will assign you to a group and give your group one or more of the combinations from the Personal Strengths Assessment in week 1. In your group analyze the key strengths and common weaknesses for your assigned combination.

(1) Record some of the joys this couple will likely experience because of their strengths;

(2) List the challenges they may face because of common weaknesses;

(3) Suggest words of wisdom you would offer this couple;

(4) For extra credit, design a bumper sticker for this couple's car!

Combination 1:   Lion and Lion

Combination 2:   Lion and Otter

Combination 3:   Lion and Golden Retriever

Combination 4:   Lion and Beaver

Combination 5:   Otter and Otter

Combination 6:   Otter and Golden Retriever

Combination 7:   Otter and Beaver

Combination 8:   Golden Retriever and Golden Retriever

Combination 9:   Golden Retriever and Beaver

Combination 10:   Beaver and Beaver

Session 2: Scripture Search

Take notes as your group discusses each passage.

Study Verse #1

Isaiah 29:16

"You have turned things around, as if the potter were the same as the clay. How can what is made say about its maker, 'He didn't make me' "? (HCSB)

Study Verse #2

Isaiah 45:9

"Woe to the one who argues with his Maker—one clay pot among many. Does clay say to the one forming it: What are you making? Or does your work [say]: 'He has no hands?' " (HCSB)

Study Verse #3

Jeremiah 18:1-4

"[This is] the word that came to Jeremiah from the LORD: 'Go down at once to the potter's house; there I will reveal My words to you.' So I went down to the potters' house, and there he was, working away at the wheel. But the jar that he was making from the clay became flawed in the potter's hand, so he made it into another jar, as it seemed right for him to do" (HCSB).

Session 3: LOVE

REQUIRES	RELINQUISHES

Session 3: Building Openness

Finish this acrostic with your group. Take notes in the space provided.

O

P

E

N

N

E

S

S

Session 3: Design the Date of the Century

What are we going to do?	
Where are we going??	
When are we going?	
Do we need child care?	
Purpose of this date?	
Evaluation: How would we rate it?	

Session 4: Masking Emotions

List masks that influence emotional intimacy. Write the likely results.

Masks	Effects of Masks on Emotional Intimacy
Examples:	
Pride	Pride doesn't admit mistakes. Spouses may refuse to display real emotion, hiding their vulnerability behind pride instead.
Deceit	Deceit erodes trust in marriage. Trust is critical to emotional intimacy.
Others?	

Session 4: Guardrails for Marriage

Take notes on these guardrails for marriage.

- **Read Signals**

- **Respond Lovingly**

- **Refresh One Another**

- **Resist Temptation**

- **Rekindle the Home Fires**

Session 5: Dragon Slayers Unite!

Read Ephesians 6:10-17.
Match the descriptions on the left
with the pieces of armor on the right.
Then, write the purpose of each piece.

Belt of Truth

Breastplate of Righteousness

Feet Shod in Peace

Shield of Faith

Helmet of Salvation

Sword of the Spirit

Session 5: Scripture Search

Take notes on these Scriptures as they are discussed in the group session.

"Deceit is in the hearts of those who plot evil, but those who promote peace have joy." Prov. 12:20

" 'I have told you these things so that in Me you may have peace. You will have suffering in this world. Be courageous! I have conquered the world.' " John 16:33

"Do what you have learned and received and heard and seen in me, and the God of peace will be with you." Phil. 4:9

" 'Peace I leave with you. My peace I give to you. I do not give to you as the world gives. Your heart must not be troubled or fearful.' " John 14:27

"So then, we must pursue what promotes peace and what builds up one another." Rom. 14:19

"No discipline seems enjoyable at the time, but painful. Later on, however, it yields the fruit of peace and righteousness to those who have been trained by it." Hebrews 12:11